WILLIAM J. BAUSCH

BREAKING TRUST

A Priest Looks at the Scandal of Sexual Abuse

TWENTY-THIRD PUBLICATIONS

185 WILLOW STREET • PO BOX 180 • MYSTIC, CT 06355
TEL: 1-800-321-0411 • FAX: 1-800-572-0788
E-MAIL: ttpubs@aol.com • www.twentythirdpublications.com

Twenty-Third Publications
A Division of Bayard
185 Willow Street
P.O. Box 180
Mystic, CT 06355
(860) 536-2611
(800) 321-0411
www.twentythirdpublications.com

ISBN:1-58595-234-6
Library of Congress Catalog Card Number:2002103866
Printed in the U.S.A.

Dedication

To the victims of my brothers

Judas, is it with a kiss that you are betraying the Son of Man?

—Lk 22:48

Contents

Introduction

For I think that God has exhibited us apostles as last of all, as though sentenced to death, because we have become a spectacle to the world, to angels and to mortals. —1 Cor 4:9

In the course of a half century, I have seen more Christian corruption than you have read of. I have tasted it. I have been reasonably corrupt myself. And yet, I love this Church, this living, pulsing, sinning people of God with a crucifying passion. Why? For all the Christian hate, I experience here a community of love. For all the institutional idiocy, I find here a tradition of reason. For all the individual repressions, I breathe here an air of freedom. For all the fear of sex, I discover here the redemption of my body. In an age so inhuman, I touch here tears of compassion. In a world so grim and humorless, I share here rich joy and earthy laughter. In the midst of death, I hear here an incomparable stress on life. For all the apparent absence of God, I sense here the real presence of Christ.

That conviction, so ably proclaimed by the noble priest, Father Walter Burghardt, has prompted this little book by another priest. Yes, indeed, as St. Paul rudely noted, the Catholic clergy has become a spectacle to all—to the angels who must weep and to us mortals who are ashamed. The revelation of widespread child sexual abuse by priests is now commonplace, although not as common as the media would have us believe. The resulting shame is a heavy burden that will be with us a long time. The Church will never be the same. And that, perhaps, as we shall see, may be the hidden grace, the seed that comes through the rotting soil. Meanwhile, until we get there, we must learn from our mistakes.

For all who hope to so learn, and especially for Catholics whose faith and trust have been deeply shaken, this small book is written. It hopes to summarize the painful story, examine the fallout, look at the lingering effects this scandal has had on us all, project a Church of the future, and finally offer a way of healing, hope, and recovery. It also will spotlight the main critical issues that are facing Catholics today, issues that were systematically kept hidden from them, but which a resilient people of God must know about and deal with.

My most fervent wish for this book is that its size may encourage people to use it for sharing sessions. Perhaps some progressive pastor will purchase copies for his people, or people themselves will do so on their own initiative. Take, say, two chapters a meeting to discuss the contents, then wrestle with the reflection questions at the end of each chapter. Prayer groups, Bible study groups, the women's and men's guilds, and just plain ad hoc groups might do this. I think a parish-wide invitation to such open forums would be most helpful and most healing. And the book at least provides topics and data, a progressive outline and some precision in terms, so the discussions don't wander into mere recrimination and mindless exchange. The premise is that the more the issues are aired the better.

In closing, I should tell you that this book was written with a heavy heart during Holy Week of 2002, in the height of the scandal. Its lingering malaise made that Holy Week unique, a time when we all, especially the clergy, experienced the passion and death of Jesus in a newer, more profound, and more personal way. To that extent, I guess, this work is a prolonged reflection arising from that week. But it is to be noted also that Easter that year was bravely if cautiously celebrated as a turning point, as the beginning of something new. It is to be hoped that by the time you read these pages that beginning has begun to blossom into a renewed Church.

ONE

Scandal

If any of you put a stumbling block before one of these little ones who believe in me, it would be better for you if a great millstone were fastened around your neck and you were drowned in the depth of the sea. —Mt 18:6

It may be hard to believe today, but once upon a time the Catholic priest was a cultural icon depicted by popular actors in countless movies. There was Bing Crosby who played the genial Father O'Malley in *Going My Way*, Humphrey Bogart who played the missionary in *The Left Hand of God*, Pat O'Brien, the gung-ho Father Duffy in *The Fighting 69th*, Gregory Peck, the stalwart priest in the *Keys of the Kingdom*, Spencer Tracy, the redoubtable Father Flanagan of Boys Town, who believed there was no such thing as a bad boy, Karl Malden, the labor priest in *On the Waterfront*, and William Gargan, the sympathetic priest in *You Only Live Once*. Characters were men. They were virile. They were dedicated. They were above life-size. They were the ones who helped make, for three consecutive years, 1943 to 1945, uplifting movies that centered admiringly on Roman Catholicism. *The Song of Bernadette*, *Going My Way*, and *Keys of the Kingdom* were nominated for thirty-four Oscars and won twelve. Indeed, after World War II, Roman Catholicism was riding high.

Fifty years later it is in disgrace. And it has been disgraced by those very same priests who brought it glory. The disgrace didn't start in the Northeast, but the dam finally burst in Boston. In January of 2002, the *Boston Globe* acquired documents showing that John Geoghan, suspended from priestly ministry in 1994 and defrocked in 1998, had been moved from one assignment to another even though it was alleged that he had molested nearly 200 children for more than thirty years. This was shocking. How could this be? The man was a pedophile. He sexually abused children. But the scandal didn't stop with that groundbreaking case.

The year after John Geoghan was defrocked, his fellow diocesan priest, Father Joseph Birmingham, died. It seems now that he was a ghastly competitor to Father Geoghan. More than thirty people have come forward to say that Father Birmingham, in his thirty-year career, molested them and other boys. The number of his victims may equal that of Father Geoghan's. He too was accused several times. Diocesan authorities were informed over the years about his crimes, but he also was consistently reassigned to parishes where he abused other boys.

Father Paul Shanley, along with Father Geoghan, is one of the more sickening cases. Known as the "street priest" for his work among drug abusers and drifters, he was dubbed as a "troubled priest" by his bishop, Cardinal Humberto Medeiros, in 1979 because of allegations of sexual misconduct with children. In fact, as far back as 1967 the archdiocese knew of such allegations against him. Shanley, alleging that he himself had been sexually abused as a teenager and later as a seminarian by a priest, has recently been arrested for raping boys during the 1980s in Massachusetts and will be extradited there.

The records show that Shanley brought the boys into the bathroom, to the rectory, and even into the confessional to molest them. He endorsed sex between men and boys and was at the 1978 conference where the North American Man-Boy Love Association was apparently created. A 1994 memo, summarizing a psychiatric report, indicated that his problems were "irreversible" and that his "pathology is beyond repair." Yet Shanley, a serial child molester, was allowed to function and to move to California where, without any notice or warning from the Archdiocese of Boston, he was permitted access to children.

How could a bishop move such abusing priests on to other children? What about the victims? The answer that emerged, in what would be a consistent pattern all over the country, was that the victims were often intimidated, bought off, sworn to secrecy and "confidentiality." They were destined to live with their guilt, shame, and emotional scars.

It need not have been that way. The bishop of Boston, in this case, Cardinal Bernard Law, should have acted differently because he and his top aides, like all the other bishops of the country, were well aware that the problem of abusive priests was not new. Though long ongoing as we now know, the evil news of clergy molestation broke publicly when, in 1985, the Rev. Gilbert Gauthe was convicted, the first case of a pedophile priest to gain national attention. Then in his late thirties, the hip priest who rode a motorcycle and wore cowboy boots admitted that he had sexually abused dozens of altar boys. The *Times* of Atlanta, a weekly newspaper, reported the case. The diocese of Lafayette, Louisiana, wound up paying millions of dollars in settlement cases and Gauthe was sentenced to twenty years in prison.

Not an aberration

Nationwide, everyone was stunned over the Gauthe case but, since it was the first such public case, everyone also hoped it would go away. As it turned out, however, that case was just the tip of the iceberg. In July of 1997, for example, a Dallas court found the Catholic diocese there had been grossly negligent in supervising Father Rudolph Kos, who had molested more than ten boys, and it awarded almost $120 million to the plaintiffs. Kos had abused boys ranging in ages from twelve to sixteen from the late 1980s to the early 1990s, molesting them hundreds of times each. One boy told the police that Father Kos had sexually molested him 550 times over seven years!

David Gagnon, now thirty-seven, was fifteen when Father Michael Doucette in Biddeford, Maine, invited him to stay over at the rectory. This was the beginning of three years of sexual victimization. In 1992 Father James Porter from Fall River, Massachusetts, was found to have abused nearly 200 victims. He too had been shifted from assignment to assignment. Father John Lenihan from Anaheim, California, publicly admitted in 1991 that he had been having "sexual encounters" with a minor. He assaulted a girl when she was fourteen, impregnated her when she was sixteen, and paid for her abortion. The military vicariate endorsed Father Robert Peebles as a reserve military officer even though the records showed he was an alcoholic and sexual abuser and had been found with an underage boy in his sleeping quarters. Former major league baseball player Tom Paciorek says that Father Gerard Shrilla molested him and his three brothers as children at St. Ladislaus school in Detroit. Thirty-five-year-old Father Robert Hands on Long Island pleaded guilty to having sex with a thirteen-year-old boy for over a year. Father Timothy Swea from Wisconsin was sentenced to jail for the abuse of a minor.

Father Lawrence Brett of Stamford, Connecticut, abused fourteen-year-old Frank Martelli. Church authorities discovered his sins in 1992 but did not report him or warn parishioners. Instead they let him minister elsewhere and in 1990, Bishop Egan, now the Cardinal archbishop of New York, reinstated him. Cardinal Egan is now under investigation for how he handled this and similar cases. Father George Cooley abused a boy in 1978. The boy's father did not press charges in return for the promise that the priest would be kept away from boys. In 1981 the priest was put in charge of altar boys, and two brothers became his next victims.

Monsignor Patrick O'Shea, adviser to former Archbishop John Quinn of San Francisco, is accused of molesting nine boys in the 1960s and '70s but he can't be tried because of the statute of limitations. Nationwide more cases of priests with multiple victims have followed: Santa Fe, New Mexico, Fall River, Massachusetts, Santa Rosa, California. Even the military hasn't been spared when, as in the case of the diocese of Dallas, a sexually abusive priest was ordered to join the army where, as a chaplain, he molested a boy. There are currently hundreds of priests across the country accused of the sexual abuse of minors. The litany seems to go on and on. Each day seems to add another name to the list. The public has been stunned at the sheer magnitude of the cases both in numbers and in depth. Some children have been molested over and over again over many years.

The flood of public accusations continues as I write this and it will continue for a while. Lawyers who are handling these cases are getting hundreds of calls a week. Emboldened by all of the publicity, victims, mostly male, are coming forward but many undoubtedly will stay in the shadows. The reason is that it is harder for males to admit molestation, to admit they were stupid enough to be taken in by a priest. If they come from a devout family, the priest was simply too exalted to be accused: it might cost you your spiritual salvation to say such a thing out loud. Anyway, back then, your parents would not believe that of dear Father Joe. One victim, Ralph Sidaway, says that when he was abused by his priest sixty-five years ago and told his mother, she smacked him around for saying such things about a holy man. In the worst of ironies, his adult son, Keith, says he was molested by his parish priest as a child, Father Rocco D'Angelo. Two generations of victims of clergy abuse!

But that reticence is disappearing quickly. Suddenly the problem is out in the open, so much so that not one of the country's 195 dioceses is without its cases. Lawyers have forced the publication of lists of clergy abusers, the vast majority of whom committed their crimes many decades ago. The numbers of those dismissed so far is staggering: ninety priests from the Archdiocese of Boston—that's almost ten percent of their current number—thirty-five in Philadelphia, three in St. Louis, two in Maine, one in Fargo, North Dakota, a half dozen or so in Pittsburgh, twelve in Los Angeles, thirteen in Trenton, New Jersey, eleven in Rhode Island. In all, some 176 priests in dozens of dioceses have so far been removed, suspended, or put on leave.

A *USA Today* survey (March 21, 2002) showed that one in eleven Catholics say they have some "personal knowledge" of sexual abuse by a priest, one in five say priests in their diocese have been accused of child sexual abuse. In other words, across the board, Catholics are aware of what they perceive to be the magnitude of the problem, and see it as widespread and longstanding. And they seem to be painfully aware that the number of cases will continue to grow. Still, as we will have occasion to repeat, the figures represent less than half of one percent of the 46,000-plus priests in the United States.

Bishops and worldwide scandals

Accusations and confessions have infiltrated the hierarchy as well. One well-placed insider says that over the past quarter century at least five U.S. bishops have been accused of sexual involvement with boys under eighteen. In each instance the bishop was deemed guilty, called on the carpet, but not removed. Information about such cases was highly restricted. More recently and more publicly, Bishop Anthony O'Connell resigned from the diocese of Palm Beach, Florida. He admitted that as rector of St. Thomas seminary in Hannibal, Missouri, he molested a student, Christopher Dixson, in the 1970s. O'Connell had a great reputation and was honored as a good teacher. But he was seducing his students. Dixson says, "It was such a tangled web of 'I love you'; 'I want to help you become a better person' even as he was taking me to bed. It was a very complex seduction."

Dixson, a resigned priest, claims three priests in the seminary abused him. And it seems that three more seminarians, all gay, have stepped forward to accuse the bishop. Recently, another former seminarian produced records showing that the bishop paid him $21,000 a month for "financial assistance." All this did not deter O'Connell from being named bishop. Ironically, he was sent to replace the previous bishop, Joseph Keith Symons, the first U.S. bishop who was forced to resign after admitting that he had sexually abused five teenage boys. The diocese continues to reel after losing two tainted bishops. Bishop G. Patrick Zeimann from Santa Rosa, California, admitted having sex with another priest who in turn was himself accused of molesting boys.

Seminaries and institutions of all kinds are also not exempt from incidents of clerical sexual abuse. The Franciscan friars of California have paid more than one million dollars for a settlement with an alleged sexual victim. The Christian Brothers from Newfoundland had to close the Mount Cashal orphanage they ran after more than twenty former residents came forward with accounts of sexual abuse. Nine brothers were convicted, thirty are facing lawsuits, and the Christian Brothers have settled out of court for an undisclosed amount.

In England, police are investigating allegations of child abuse against a former chaplain, Father David Martin, at a Catholic school attended by Prime Minister Blair's two eldest sons. In France, about thirty priests have been convicted in recent years for pedophile acts and eleven are in prison. A sixty-three-year-old Swiss priest is in custody on suspicion of sexually abusing children. A study in Spain claims that sixty percent of its priests are sexually active and from a sample of 354 priests who are sexually active, twenty-six percent are active with minors. A random sample of Catholic clergy in South Africa revealed that approximately forty-five percent of priests reported being sexually active with someone.

In Poland Archbishop Juliusz Paetz has been accused of homosexual advances and of molesting seminarians, and has resigned. In Austria Cardinal Hans Hermann Groer was forced into retirement after he was accused of molesting seminarians. There is no doubt that the scandal of sexual abuse will, sooner or later, reach the Vatican. Two years ago Marco Polti, an Italian author who had co-written a book on the present pope with American Carl Bernstein, published a book entitled *La Confessione*, which revealed a whole network of homosexual priests who are active in the Italian Church and its seminaries.

In Ireland, Bishop Brendan Comiskey resigned because he protected a sexually abusing priest, Father Sean Fortune, who assaulted dozens of boys and who committed suicide in 1999 before his trial. The bishop himself also came under scrutiny because he was treated for alcoholism and visited Thailand, where he stayed at a hotel used by male prostitutes. There was also an accusation that Ireland's late archbishop was a pedophile, plus the publication of the book *Suffer the Little Children* and its spin-off TV documentary enumerating incidents of sexual and physical abuse in Church-run institutions. These have sent shock waves throughout that country. In January of 2002, the Catholic Church in Ireland agreed to a landmark $110 million payment to children abused by clergy over decades. More than twenty priests and brothers have been convicted of molesting children. Along with the presence of the Celtic Tiger (economic prosperity), these scandals have determined the identity of Ireland today as a post-Catholic country.

A.W. Richard Sipe and his colleague, Dr. Leo Bartemeir, who have done a huge amount of research on clerical abusers, estimated about thirty years ago that about six percent of all Catholic priests acted out sexually with minors. Father Andrew Greeley estimates between five and seven percent. Greeley further estimates this figure to be between 10,000 to 15,000 victims of sexual abuse by Catholic priests and religious in the United States. Again, while these numbers remain statistically moderate compared to non-clergy, they are still unacceptable.

The stories horrify us: altar boys lured into bed by priests, children forced to perform oral sex. The hurt, degradation, and pain are fathomless. We are profoundly and grievously wounded to learn that our priests entrusted with our children have betrayed them. We are more than angry to learn that our bishops used our money to pay off victims. We find ourselves moving from revulsion to shock to anger and finally to numbness.

There is a picture that continues to haunt the collective Catholic mind. It's a full-page photograph in *Time* magazine (April 2, 2002) showing Father Rudy Kos standing next to twelve-year-old Jay Lemberger. Jay is dressed in his white altar boy's robe, smiling the innocent boyish smile of a twelve year old. Father Kos is in his clerics. Father Kos got three life sentences for abusing Jay and others like him. Jay shot himself dead at the age of twenty-one.

Questions for discussion

1. Do you know of any priest who has been accused of sexually molesting minors?

2. Did this happen in your own parish? How did the diocese handle the situation? How did the people? Did the diocese send a task force or did the bishop come to speak to the parish?

3 What are your feelings about the news of so many trusted priests being charged with sexual abuse?

4. What makes you most angry about this whole situation?

TWO

Cover-up

Beware of false prophets who come to you in sheep's clothing but inwardly are ravenous wolves. —Mt 7:15

As long ago as 1985, when the Gauthe case from Louisiana was shocking the nation, the liberal Catholic newspaper, the *National Catholic Reporter*, was printing accounts of sexual abuse by priests. *NCR* was also the first national publication to run Jason Berry's ground-breaking examination of the crisis. Even *The Wanderer*, a conservative newspaper far removed from the liberalism of the *Reporter*, also helped expose abuse related scandals.

There was no excuse, then, for bishops on either side of the liberal-conservative spectrum not to be alert. In fact the *National Catholic Reporter* repeatedly called for Church authorities to develop means to protect children from predator priests. The paper again repeated its appeal in 1988. It went unheeded, at least in any serious way. In 1985, canon lawyer Father Thomas Doyle, at the Vatican embassy in Washington, had drafted a one-hundred-page report advising that offenders be kept apart from children, that the victims be helped, and, most of all, that the public be told the truth. He then added his opinion that a far-reaching and serious problem was in fact at the doorstep, and he predicted that a billion dollars in legal claims might be brought against the Church. He went unheeded. Unfortunately, he was right on the mark.

From 1962 to 1982, Cardinal John Cody was the archbishop of Chicago. During his tenure he learned of a pedophiliac ring of priests in Wisconsin who were passing around their victims to one another. When the press got wind of this information, Cody used his clout to kill the story. If only the Church had openly faced the problem then! Ironically, in another part of Chicago, in October of 1992, a woman who had been abused by her minister convened a gathering of victims ("survivors" they like to call themselves) of sexual abuse by clergy. (Later this and other groups would be connected in a loose network now known as LINKUP.) These were mainstream, moderate, traditional folk.

For three days they listened to each other's stories and listened to experts. The feelings of all were summed up by Jeanne Miller whose son had been molested by Father Richard Mayer more than a decade ago: "It is a violation of trust that reaches further into the psyche than any other kind of breach." All their stories had a common refrain: denial by the local bishop, a reshuffling of the abusing priest, discrediting the accuser, and being made to swear to secrecy. In a word, the Church stonewalled.

The bishops were stirring a bit with each new scandal but failed to see the seriousness and magnitude of the problem. The National Council of Catholic Bishops in 1982 started some initial investigations into the problem and increased its inquiries in 1984. After the Gauthe case, they began drafting universal procedures and issued a brief statement on child molestation claims in November of 1989. In 1992 the bishops got around to forming a subcommittee on sexual abuse chaired by Father Canice Connors, OFM, and convened a think tank in February of 1993. They also formed an ad hoc committee on clergy sexual abuse and, finally, in November of 1994 issued the first of three volumes of *Restoring Trust.*

But it was too little and too late. As one priest scholar said, "Any bishop who made this mistake [of paying off victims] before 1985 I think is forgivable because there was great ignorance and naivete. But in 1985 when the Louisiana case blew up, that had to be the beginning of a wake-up call." The bishops, then, were well aware of sex abuses among their priests. In the unrelenting glare of public scrutiny the bishops are now struggling to catch up and wake up. In March of this year (2002), after a three-day meeting in Washington, DC, the committee added the problem of clergy sexual abuse of minors to the agenda of their upcoming meeting in Dallas, Texas during June. "We recognize our responsibility as bishops to address this problem more effectively," they said. The bishops, repeating their 1992 principles, also pledged to act promptly on allegations of sexual misconduct by their priests, comply with civil laws on reporting sex abuse cases, reach out to the victims and their families, and "deal as openly as possible with the members of the community."

Secrecy and stonewalling

But it wasn't always so. Three major charges brought against the bishops tell why. First, there is the charge that there has been undue secrecy and cover-up in these matters. The truth is that sexual activity among priests was always an open secret. Some priests were having sex with adults or minors; to some degree, this was taken for granted and winked at. It was a secret world of abuse known to the hierarchy, but since there was no open public crisis, such abuse was viewed as merely human weakness. Besides, above all, scandal was to be avoided. The bishops also knew that some seminary faculty members were abusing students. It is to be further noted that in 1976 the Servants of the Paraclete in New Mexico opened up what was perhaps the first program in the world specifically to treat the psychosexual disorders of priests and religious, including the sexual abuse of minors. The scope of the problem was therefore obviously well-known by the bishops. Still, they would not air the problems. They obviously thought Dryden was right:

For secrets are edged tools,
And must be kept from children and from fools.

The children were the unsuspecting victims exposed to recycled abusers and the fools were evidently the Catholic people who were to be "protected."

So secrecy was the order of the day. People were neither to be told nor warned lest they be scandalized. Better not to let the public know. Case after case was kept hidden. Even the growing public exposure brought no attempts at honesty and openness. Dioceses fell into a pattern of denial and outright deception. It was a virtual culture of secrecy, deference, and self-protecting strategies. At all costs the Church was to be protected, and survivor's families were admonished not to put forth any publicity that would harm it. When cases were brought up, the local bishop was in effect prosecutor, judge, and jury. No civil official was consulted. Worse, no parish was warned they were getting an abusive priest. Revelations of sexual abuse were to be kept in their domain, for it was, in their eyes, a moral failure and a religious matter. And yet the bishops were only following Rome, which tends to see sexual abuse in terms of a moral violation of celibacy, not in terms of the crime that it is.

The use of secrecy and stonewalling, in and of themselves, should not surprise us. Everyone, from individuals to corporations, initially denies hostile allegations and tries to protect the good name of the family or the institution. Banks, for example, quietly dismiss employees who embezzle rather than risk public prosecution so that its customers will not get alarmed and think their money is in danger. Presidents of countries, like Bill Clinton, and corporations like Enron routinely employ the talents of "spin doctors" and the offices of the multibillion-dollar image industry to hide or fudge unsavory or damaging charges. Cover-ups by government agencies, the police, and the military are standard fare. It has been common practice to allow the alcoholic or sexually compromised congressman, judge, doctor, and movie star to go off to a private institution and be returned to work without any publicity about their failings.

H.R. Haldeman's White House diaries revealed that the venerable Billy Graham joined President Nixon in making anti-Semitic remarks. In May of 1994, Graham stonewalled and denied it. "Those are not my words," he proclaimed loudly. "I have never talked publicly or privately about the Jewish people, including conversations with President Nixon, except in the most positive terms." But when the tapes from Nixon's oval office were released eight years later, we can hear Graham right there denigrating the Jews far more than what was noted in Halderman's book. Graham has since issued a four-sentence apology. But we can sympathize with his initial denial and cover-up because he wants us to embrace the enormous good he has done. And we should.

Martin Luther King, Jr., was sexually unfaithful to his wife; the FBI taped numerous episodes of sexual encounters in King's hotel rooms. Ralph Abernathy has revealed that King carried on extramarital affairs right up until the eve of his death. King also plagiarized, a serious offense. He inserted long sections lifted without credit from other sources into his graduate school thesis, his writings, and sometimes even his speeches. Initially his followers denied all this, insisting such things were lies issued by his detractors. That was understandable. They didn't want such revelations to taint the undeniable heroism of the man or the powerful legacy he has left.

The media itself, so eager to reveal the sins of others, closes ranks and fudges when their members or news organizations err or are revealed as prejudiced or managing or distorting the news. Bestselling books, like Bernard Goldberg's *Bias* or William McGowan's *Coloring the News,* Jerry Bledsoe's *Death by Journalism* and Tammy Bruce's *The New Thought Police: Inside the Left's Assault on Free Speech and Free Minds,* expose the stonewalling. This preamble is not to excuse the Church but to show how far it has succumbed to the values and mentality of the modern corporation. For the dioceses did deny, minimize, and cover up abuse. Dioceses were driven to use legal stratagems and file barrages of legal motions. They trotted out the claims that too much time had passed, that the Church was shielded by the First Amendment protection of religious freedom; that the diocese was not liable because a priest abusing the children was not working on behalf of the diocese but rather the local Church.

The National Conference of Catholic Bishops took the same stance: the Conference couldn't do much, it protested, because it had no authority to impose on individual autonomous dioceses. But that excuse rang hollow considering how the Conference had passed all kinds of rules for every diocese concerning the liturgy, mandating when people should stand or kneel and so on. All were dubious, all unworthy claims. Add to this the secret financial settlements and sealed documents and you have exactly the approach used by corporations. Of course, this approach is backfiring as documents are unsealed revealing that the Church did indeed know about clergy sexual abuse and is therefore liable as an institution and may be forced to pay punitive damages.

Clerical roulette

Second, there is the serious charge, fully justified, that abusive priests were protected and simply moved around. This rankles and disturbs people most. The furor over the Boston case involving John Geoghan was precisely that Geoghan, known by Cardinal Law and his aides to have molested boys, was nevertheless moved to other places where he repeated his molestation. Yet this unconscionable and horrific practice was common in every diocese. To give the bishops their due, the medical and psychiatric understandings of pedophilia, as we shall see later, were quite primitive and limited.

The medical community thought some basic treatment would contain the problem and believed in a psychological cure. The Church community—whose business, after all, is redemption, thought that repentance and prayer would handle it. Still, there was growing evidence that pedophilia was a special illness, akin to alcoholism, which meant that it could only be contained not cured. It was wrong, utterly wrong, to simply transfer a known child abuser to another assignment where children were present. Furthermore, because of the almost paranoid secrecy, sometimes abusive priests were recycled to other dioceses without any warning to a new parish or school. With this in mind, people have every right to be outraged.

The third charge is against the Church's handling of the victims and their families. Some were treated kindly, but, for the most part, they were sometimes made to seem the perpetrators. They were paid off, made to sign confidentiality papers, and given no special care or treatment. (Victims are more and more making public their own cases, in spite of confidentiality agreements, knowing that they stand little chance of legal action if they do so). They were frequently intimidated. I personally know of one case where a family threatened to sue the diocese over the sexual abuse of their son and was told that they would be excommunicated if they did so.

Bishops sometimes blamed the victim and were often hostile to the family, according to Barbara Blaine of the Survivors' Network of Those Abused by Priests (S.N.A.P.), a Chicago-based national organization of nearly 500 people who have been molested by Catholic clergy. She cites cases where bishops have countersued families who have taken legal action against priests (defamation of character, they said), publicly counterattacked survivors, and even revealed their names, HIV status, and sexual orientation. A bishop from the Midwest publicly stated, "Young boys recover from this type of thing very quickly if people don't make a big deal out of it."

At times, it was suggested that the victims played a role in the abuse. One survivor, Dennis Gaboury, speaking to large group of Catholic bishops a few years ago, said, "I want you to understand. We are not your enemies. We are your last best hope." Yet more than once, he said, he was accused of "not believing in the healing power of God." In general the abused and their families were often deceived, confused, ignored, or discouraged. They were given incomplete or misleading information that served the Church's interest rather than the victim's. It is no surprise to note that survivors became legally and politically involved almost always after having been rebuffed by Church leadership. (At this point, one can't help but think, "You can tell that bishops don't have children or grandchildren.")

Cynics have noted a double standard here. When allegations are brought against a Catholic schoolteacher, there is instant and swift reaction. The diocese notifies the legal authorities. In days, if not hours, the teacher is removed. The public relations folk assure the parents and the public about all the effort being made to "protect our children." Further contact with the offending teacher and his or her family is cut off. Public meetings are held. Case is closed. Yet nothing like this happens when a priest is accused.

So, there we are. The record is not good for a Church that professes to teach compassion for "the least of the brethren." What is perhaps most appalling to some is that bishops have become such bureaucrats that normal human instincts have been buried. And it should be noted that in the past, even when some bishops did bring cases of erring priests to Rome in order to expel them, Rome balked. Moreover, in the present crisis Rome continues to be conspicuously silent. It has not (as of this writing) forced Cardinal Law or any other prelate out of office.

Insular and preoccupied with matters elsewhere, Rome seemed to have little sense of the gravity of the situation here and tended to see the present crisis as an American problem, part of our dreadful sexual revolution. Many read Rome's inaction as an indication that it was not serious about healing the wounds caused by the scandal. It was only when he finally sensed that the situation was really getting out of hand that the pope, in an unusual move, summoned all of the American cardinals and the president of the U.S. Bishops' Conference to Rome for a special emergency meeting to discuss the matter.

The first reaction to the revelations of the abused child or adolescent should be one of utter shock. The victim should be embraced with tears and longing, while repeating over and over again, "I'm so sorry. I'm so sorry! How could this have happened? I'm so sorry!" But, like the rest of the world, the dioceses sent chancellors, lawyers, and crisis management personnel as front runners and resorted to unworthy tactics to protect the good name of the Church. The result of this is that now the Church has a bad name; Holy Mother Church is stained with sin. Shakespeare's hand-rubbing Lady Macbeth comes to mind, of whom the doctor remarks:

> Foul whisperings are abroad. Unnatural deeds
> Do breed unnatural troubles; infected minds
> To their deaf pillows will discharge their secrets;
> More needs she the divine than the physician.
> God, God, forgive us all!

> —Macbeth, Act V, Scene I

Questions for discussion

1. Do you think there has been a cover-up in the Church regarding sexual abuse?

2. Do you think any bishop involved in a cover-up who failed to act should resign?

3. Were you aware of cases and warnings concerning sexual abuse before the Boston scandal?

4. If you were a bishop, how would you have handled allegations of sexual abuse?

5. What are your feelings about the victims? the perpetrators?

THREE

The Sins of
the Fathers

*The parents have eaten sour grapes and the children's teeth
are set on edge.* —Jer 31:29

There are, as always, unintended and undesirable consequences
when the reform of a bad situation takes place. Some such consequences should be corrected. Others simply have to persist as the
price to be paid by the innocent for the crimes of the guilty. Let's
list some of them.

Loss of trust

First, there is loss of trust in the Church and the loss of respect. The
Church has lost its moral capital. How can people listen seriously
to the Church's teaching on abortion and chastity when its priests
are unchaste? How can people take the Church's admirable teachings on social justice to heart when it has been unjust to pedophile
victims? How can the Church's stance as a moral leader endure in
the face of the scandals? How can people give credence to the
Church's teaching on family life, on the care and the education of
children, when it let its own children be violated?

As for respect, the press has relentlessly paraded the sins of the
Church before the public. The mainstream magazines and newspapers have made the scandal daily front-page fare, and the
tabloid magazines and newspapers have delighted in revealing
first-person horror stories. The political cartoonists have had a field

day pillorying priests and bishops with cartoons ranging from the vulgar to the salacious. The sins of the priests and the "corruption" of the Catholic Church have become the scandal *de jour.* The once vaunted respect accorded to the Church has evaporated.

Loss of income

Second, there is the loss of income. Some parishioners are showing their disgust and dissatisfaction with the scandals by withholding money. They say that they don't want their contributions to go to paying off the victims of abusive priests. Anger is so strong that, in the area around Boston, for example, contributions to Catholic Charities, an organization that in fact has little official connection with the Church, have noticeably fallen off. Catholic Charities gets only two percent of its revenue from the Church; sixty percent of the people it serves are not Catholic. No matter. People see the word "Catholic" and withhold their money. As one spokeswoman for Catholic Charities said, "People are calling and saying things like, 'We're not going to give to anything with "Catholic" in the name.'"

Others, like well-known theologian Lisa Sowle Cahill, publicly recommend withholding contributions to diocesan and Vatican organizations as a way of pressuring the hierarchy to make changes. All this, unfortunately, comes at a time when the Church is paying out millions and millions of dollars in lawsuits and is in deep debt. Some dioceses are near bankruptcy and others are being forced to borrow heavily. To add to the financial woes, insurance companies often decline to cover the cost of the multi-million-dollar lawsuits brought against the Church. Before all this scandal dioceses were able to obtain liability insurance for as much as $50 million, but the insurance companies are saying that the molestation actions were deliberate and not covered. Moreover, they are raising their premiums.

Call for resignation

Third, there is the call for some members of the clergy and hierarchy to resign, especially those who were in any way involved in the protection of pedophiles. The call, as you might suspect, has been particularly strong in Boston where people have picketed Cardinal Law, asking him to quit. Sixty-one percent of the Catholics polled in his archdiocese agree that he should resign, although he has publicly stated that he will not. On Easter Sunday protestors carried signs before the cathedral bearing such slogans as "House of Rape," "Cardinal Law Resign," and "Stop Crucifying Us." Catholic politicians are ignoring him. The students at Boston College do not want him at their commencement exercises. Even conservative people favorable to the Church, like former Education Secretary William Bennett, John Leo, and William Buckley, are asking for the removal of the Cardinal. In his inimitable way, Buckley wrote in the *National Review*,

> The critical concern should have been to get children out of harm's way. He didn't do that....One can feel with great sorrow and understanding the derangement of the arsonist, but one does not send him back into the forest.

The pressure is tremendous. Yet, this poses a dilemma. For a bishop or cardinal to resign is quite damaging to the Church since their tenure is often seen as a lifetime commitment to the institutional Church. Any resignation, therefore, is perceived not as a flaw in the person, but as a flaw in the Church itself. Still others, even some of the alleged victims, think the Cardinal should stay. Then there are those who want the Cardinal and other bishops to do more than quit. They want them charged with criminal negligence and sent to jail. We may yet see the spectacle of a Catholic cardinal handcuffed and brought to trial and sent to prison. Prosecutors are already convening grand juries to investigate child sex allegations against priests. Archbishop Daniel Pilarczyk of Cincinnati, the former president of the National Conference of Catholic Bishops, is the first American archbishop to be subpoenaed to appear before a grand jury. He won't be the last.

There are those, says Jeffery Anderson, a lawyer from St. Paul, Minnesota, who has filed suits for hundreds of people who say they have been abused, who are convinced that the abuse won't stop "until a bishop hears the clang of a prison door behind him." Courts are going along. They are systematically rejecting the argument that the First Amendment shields churches from lawsuits accusing clergy of sexual abuse. Furthermore, lawyers, in a federal lawsuit, are gearing up to sue all the U.S. bishops of conspiring to cover up sexual abuse. They have even filed a suit against the Vatican and the pope. They are citing the Racketeer Influenced and Corrupt Organizations Act (RICO) which was written to combat organized crime but can also cover civil cases that involve a "pattern" of illegal activity. The bishops and the Vatican stand accused of engaging in a "criminal network" of conspiracy to conceal abuse.

In fact, prosecutors have gotten quite aggressive and, with unprecedented vigor, they are finding ways to chip away at statute of limitations laws for sex abusers. Buoyed by the collection of large civil settlements and an aroused public, lawyers are consistently forcing bishops through court orders to release lists of names of accused priests which, in some instances, go back as far as seventy-five years. No longer intimidated by the Church, if they ever were, lawyers are after the Church in full force, and we will see years of litigation to come. One lawyer has collected some 1,200 names of priests accused of sex crimes and only 120 of those, she found, have ever had criminal charges brought against them; fewer than eighty have served time in prison. She and other lawyers are out to change that.

Pain of the people

Fourth, there is the palatable pain of the people. I don't mean just Catholics in general, but the people immediately affected. I'm looking at a news report that tells of a pastor who was suspended in Cleveland, Ohio, over allegations that he had sexually abused children. The announcement left the people stunned. "It came as a shock to all of us. He was an outstanding pastor and had done so much," said one parishioner. That's what I mean. A talented man, a real leader, a good priest as far as anyone could tell—and now he is in disgrace and gone from their midst.

Imagine if that were your own pastor. Imagine the shock, the disbelief, and the letdown. How do you handle it? What do you tell the children? What about all the things he started? Who will replace him? Will you be able to trust him again? If the departed pastor was a close friend, a confidant, how do you react? On every level, the hurt to the parish community is incalculable. It's like a sudden and unexpected death in the family. It is only to be hoped that a diocese will quickly train and dispatch bereavement ministers to guide the parish through its loss, its time of mourning.

Public scandal

Fifth, there is the unavoidable and inevitable seedy side of public scandals. The glare of publicity on Catholic priests' sins has been unrelenting. Every major newspaper and magazine has had front page coverage. And no doubt we deserve the "slings and arrows of outrageous fortune." There is almost no one left on the globe who does not know of the Church's disgrace; the mantle of shame will hang around Catholic shoulders for a long time to come.

I must hasten to add, however, that, by and large, the mainstream newspapers and magazines have been even-handed and fair: The *New York Times* (no friend of the policies of the Church), *Time* magazine, *U.S. News and World Report*, and others have been thorough, fair, and balanced in their coverage. The talk shows like *Larry King Live*, *Oprah*, *The O'Reilly Factor*, and others have had a field day as the victims and their lawyers make the rounds. Every newscast has had its pedophile priest segment and, for the most part, has tried to be balanced. But they have gone on and on and on replacing the O.J. Simpson, Jon Benet Ramsey, and Chandra Levy marathons.

The tabloids, as expected, have gone forward full throttle. Sleazy TV shows like Howard Stern's and the iconoclastic *Saturday Night Live* have pilloried the Church. Others trot out the distasteful jokes: "Father Doyle needs an altar boy today." "Yeah, well, he does go through them." We can expect the inevitable books, made-for-television movies, perhaps even a mini-series. Of course, the Catholic priest, with his special vows and mystique, has always been irresistible to the lust-and-betrayal soap opera genre. Soap opera priests, you notice, are usually hunks—often shown in shorts or jogging outfits—who are struggling with their vows.

New dramas are in the offing. ABC's *The Chosen* depicts a former seminarian who, in his search for the spiritual, finds the Church an obstacle and the hierarchy both irrelevant and jaded.

The clear message is: if you're going to get spirituality, you're going to get it outside the Church. Another prospective series is *Father Lefty*, about a hip Miami guy in shorts. This series will push the pedophile envelope. The well-regarded *Law and Order* series features a diocesan cover-up of a top-ranking priest pedophile. *The Sopranos* is ready to mock the scandal on its series. David Letterman has already sprinkled his monologue with jokes about the scandal. We can expect television to keep alive the "corruption" of the hierarchy and the "sins" of the priests for a long time until they become stereotypes.

Then there are false accusations. There is extortion. In Nebraska, the diocese of Lincoln received a letter demanding $2,000,000 from four men threatening to go public with allegations of sexual abuse at the hand of a priest in 1978. Unscrupulous people have invaded the privacy of Cardinal Roger Mahony of Los Angeles by stealing his private e-mail messages and reading them over the air. Where there is big money to be had unscrupulous people and greedy lawyers will never be far behind and it will become increasingly difficult, in the glare of such intensive coverage, to separate fact from fiction.

And there are, as there always have been, those who hate the Church for many personal and ideological reasons. The prochoice people would like to see Cardinal Law brought down because he has been so outspokenly prolife. The hedonist group and those who are now pushing for the rights of teenagers to have "a satisfying, consensual sex life" would like to see a Church that speaks out about chastity and respect labeled as degenerate. Certain professors who have successfully inculcated moral relativism and functional nihilism would like to see a Church that talks about objective morality and eternal values discredited. Radical feminists would love to dance on the Church's grave. Act-up, the activist gay group, would like to revisit the cathedrals with renewed vigor and scatter condoms. Civil libertarians would like to strip the Church of all privileges and close the Catholic schools.

The point is that we can't be so naïve as not to think that this present crisis is not good news to many with vested interests, many who wish to destroy a Church that remains one of the few institutions left willing to say no. Some commentators could not resist pointing out the irony of a sex-saturated culture scolding the Church for being too forgiving of sexual misbehavior and the hubris of a society that tolerates and promotes anything and everything, screaming for zero tolerance. Whatever. The scandal strengthens all their hands. But, we gave it to them. They did not invent it.

Diminishment of power and influence

Sixth, the scandals have diminished the Church's moral power and influence in the political arena. This is a devastating fallout. Taking advantage of the Church's weakness and its current distraction, legislators, formerly kept at bay, have lost no time in passing laws hostile to Church teaching. For example, lawmakers in Massachusetts and New York—two places where the scandals are raging most strongly—have approved bills requiring institutions affiliated with the Church to cover prescription birth control in health insurance policies for many employees. Catholic lobbyists in the past have fought successfully to keep this from happening. They are no longer successful.

The truth is that the Church, due to the scandals, has lost its political clout. As someone said, it's hard to make a moral argument for birth control when the front pages are screaming with news of moral turpitude. Legislatures are also poised to require Church leaders to report all illegal sexual activity by the clergy, a measure that would never have been proposed until recently. In Connecticut the state House of Representatives recently approved a bill that would require priests to break the seal of confession if they learned of a crime there. This is a far cry from the legendary lore of priests, under the worst pressures and even torture, would never reveal anything in confession.

Some of you may remember the old movie *I Confess,* starring Montgomery Clift: where an innocent person almost went to the chair because Clift, a priest, could not reveal the real killer, who had confessed to him. We can expect that the legal demands that Catholic hospitals perform abortions will gain momentum. There is no doubt that the moral authority of the bishops has been compromised.

Loss of clergy

Seventh, the clerical pool will further shrink precisely at the time when we can ill afford to lose men. As we shall see in detail later, in a time when there is a severe priest shortage, vocations will further decline. Some young men who were thinking of becoming priests are having second thoughts now. Who can blame them? As one young man said, "At one time I actually thought about becoming a priest. Now, I'm not going to even set foot in the Catholic Church until they stop ordaining perverts."

Finally, and this deserves separate consideration in the following chapter, the fallout, the impact on the priests themselves has been searing.

These, then, are but some of the results of a scandal that keeps on growing, the results of the failure of good men to do the right thing, the aftermath of those who put the institution first and people second. We will have to live with such fallout for a while and brace ourselves for new unsavory revelations—at least until reformation and healing take place and, from the ashes of shame, a new Church emerges.

Questions for discussion

1. The Church has lost its moral capital. Discuss this statement.

2. Would you withhold your contributions to your parish by way of protest? to the diocese? to charities associated with the Church, like Peter's Pence?

3. Have you come across nasty remarks about priests on television? How does this make you feel?

4. What is the latest scandal you have heard about?

FOUR

Perspectives

First take the log out of your own eye, and then you will see
clearly to take the speck out of your neighbor's eye.

—Mt 7:5

Have you heard the story of the young secretary who had just gotten engaged? She came to the office the next day, but nobody noticed her ring. She preened and posed, held out her arm, but still no one noticed. Finally, in desperation, she announced in a loud voice: "My, it's warm in here. I think I'll take off my engagement ring!"

In this and the next two chapters I feel like that young lady. I want you to notice things that got lost in the hype of the media and to think about things in spite of your real anger and hateful feelings. There is no attempt here to excuse or whitewash the bishops, but there is an attempt to state that, if we really want to see the whole picture, there are certain perspectives to be considered.

First, there is the statistical reality that the number of clergy sexual perpetrators is quite small; for example, in the twenty years between 1960 and 1980, when many of the abuse cases came to light, there were about 150,000 Catholic priests and religious in our country. During that time there were about 500 reported (though not all proved) cases of abuse, which means such cases involved three-tenths of a percent of the clergy and religious. Also, most of these cases involved fifteen to seventeen-year-old boys. Since not all cases were substantiated, then the percentage is even lower.

One study done by the University of Santa Clara in 1999 estimated that five percent of Catholic priests have inclinations to pedophilia, compared to five percent of Protestant ministers and eight percent of the general population. These statistics are important to know not by way of excuse but to counter the widespread impression that the molestation of minors is an exclusively Catholic clergy problem. As prosecutor Michael Allen from Cincinnati who is pursuing criminal cases against the clergy admits, "It's such a small minority of priests who offended, and a very noble vocation is suffering." Fortunately the public, both Catholic and non-Catholic, appreciate this fact. In a recent New York *Times*/CBS poll (released on May 3, 2002) a majority said that the problem was limited to "a few or hardly any priests."

No more Father O'Malley

Second, in spite of so small a number of offenders, nevertheless the current 350 bishops and 46,000 priests in the United States are all under a cloud of suspicion, and any fair perspective says they shouldn't be. You should know that, tainted by association, the good ones feel shame, embarrassment, anger, and hurt. They are afraid to get too close to the youngsters who need them, and so the youngsters get a double whammy.

Did you ever think of that? It's a very fractured world in which these youngsters live. Half of them have experienced the divorce of their parents. Many have two busy career parents, are emotionally abandoned, and are routinely sub-contracted out. They have little supervision, and their minds and their morals are morally shaped daily by a relentless consumerist society. They are early sexualized by the soft and hard pornography of advertising and television. Drugs beckon.

Therefore they cherish more than ever the private moment when Father is driving them home and they get up the courage to say, "Father, can I ask you something?" They savor the encouraging arm around the shoulder, especially if they have no father. They relish a touch that is not hostile and angry but affirming. But, alas, no more. Who is the priest who will risk that? And both sides lose out: the children who need a confidant and role model and the priest who feels their need.

One priest who works in a Latino parish says that when a little kid comes up to hug you, you pull back. And that is sad because the kid most likely needs a hug. At times, as I have frequently experienced, the little kids say, "There goes God" and they would love to hug "God" but "God" pauses in anguish: does "God" embrace them or push them away?

Most priests are good, holy, and loving pastors. They cherish their people and are proud when some kid says he would like to be just like him. But now they feel restrained. They feel the pain of the priesthood betrayed. They sense it when even good parishioners look at them differently. And they live in fear that *they* may be falsely accused. They know that one unproven accusation is enough to get their picture plastered across the front page. They are aware of the *USA Today* poll that shows that eighty-three percent of Catholics are likely to believe the accusation when a priest is accused of child sexual abuse. Innocent clergy feel deeply the injustice of that. No one seems to realize that, in the hysteria of the moment, justice is often set aside—not just justice for the victims, but often justice for the accused.

Who doesn't recall, for example, the unending media barrage of the early nineties when every newspaper, magazine, and TV newscast recounted the scandal of child sex abuse at day care centers? People who had "recovered memories" stepped forward and brought forth all kinds of lurid accusations. Psychologists were on television with little children and little dolls to illustrate what had happened. Talk show hosts were properly horrified, and so was the public. The day care people were humiliated and vilified. Their photographs were all over the papers. There were few level heads.

Well, as we know, the accusations turned out to be largely false. The use of "recovered memory" has become so problematic that it has spawned literally tons of books, papers, and monographs concerning its legal, ethical, and psychological aspects, with professionals vehemently lining up on either side of the reliability question. Who does not remember the accusation of sexual abuse brought against the late Cardinal Bernardin of Chicago with CNN giving a full exposé of the whole sordid affair? The accuser finally admitted that his recovered memory was faulty: the Cardinal was innocent.

Old cases

Third, the cases you have been hearing and reading about are old. Think about it. The perpetrators are in their fifties, sixties, and seventies. You hardly hear of any clergy sexual abusers in the last fifteen years—and, in these days of high publicity and high compensations, they would surely come forward. The truth is that the bad conduct occurred anywhere from fifteen to thirty or more years ago, and the majority of offenders have long since died or retired or been removed from the active priesthood. The reason no new cases have surfaced is that the bishops have in fact acted on guidelines honed in the 1990s and, even though applied unevenly throughout the country's 195 dioceses, they did and have acted since that time.

Once again, most of the sexual abuse cases happened in the past. This does not mean that we should not remember these shameful incidents or dismiss the memories of the terrible violations of trust and the breach of relationships any more than we should forget that we once imprisoned the Japanese, committed atrocities in Vietnam, did medical experiments on prisoners, and held slaves. It *does* mean that we have moved on, that we have changed, that we have, for example, struck down Jim Crow laws.

In the same way, the bishops who acted irresponsibly before 1990, have by and large acted responsibly in the past fifteen years as is obvious from the small number of cases since then. Prior to the 1990s, it took a lot of scandal, large payments, and the courage of victims to finally get the bishops moving. But little by little, they did move. They gathered in meetings and workshops, listened to the experts, and tightened up seminary screening. Many did take action. Not all, but many did and, as I said, the proof is in the tiny incidents that have occurred since the early 1990s.

What I am saying is that, while it took too long and was often too late, the record does show that, prior to all the current exposure, the bishops were not all indifferent and callous, but voluntarily acted and often acted effectively. You would get the impression that a seething cesspool of abuse was percolating unchecked right up to the moment of the Boston exposure. But this is not so. Bishop Wuerl of Pittsburgh and the late Cardinal

Bernardin of Chicago are good examples of prelates who, in 1991 and 1992, put in concrete measures to deal with clergy sexual abuse.

In presenting this, I am trying to counter the media impression that nothing was done prior to the Boston exposé, no action was taken, and no bishop was concerned. But something really did change and once more you have to notice that we are largely dealing with old-time abusers, which caused even *Time* magazine to confess, "Almost every case on record happened years ago."

Regrettably, we have to admit that the momentum of these creative years was lost. This was due largely to that false accusation made in November 1993 (and withdrawn some four months later) against Cardinal Bernardin. Lawyer Stephen Rubino, much in the news today, was the one who orchestrated the accusation with CNN to gain massive news coverage. When the charges proved to be embarrassingly false, then some leading critics of the bishops' previous inaction who had jumped on the media bandwagon badly lost their credibility. The media itself was embarrassed and, as a result, the pressure, unfortunately, was off the bishops to sustain and pursue more cases and a more firm policy.

Fourth, we spoke of the bishops' secrecy in chapter two. Indeed, there was unnecessary secrecy; and more up-front honesty would have been better. The bishops overall acted indecisively by not pursuing a well-defined national policy on sexual abuse and settlements, and how and when they should reveal the truth. Secrecy was sometimes an attempt to save face, deceive, and hide unpleasant facts. But perspective says not all the time. There's another side to the secrecy, which is that very often the use of secrecy was not the Church's choice but the victim's. As Peter Steinfels, writing in *Commonweal* (April 19, 2002) states:

> Quiet settlements and sealed court records are not necessarily sinister. One legal expert who has worked on Church matters for decades told me, "Eighty percent of the time it was victims who asked for confidentiality." "How do you know?" I asked in return. "Fifteen years of talking to diocesan attorneys," he said. This man is someone I respect. He is right to point out that many settlements have been sealed to protect

the victim's reputation rather than the Church's. But in the present climate, his testimony and that of diocesan attorneys just won't suffice. He and they will not be seen as disinterested. In fact, keeping settlements secret, a fairly standard legal step, has probably been the mutual preference of Church officials and victims in many cases.

Many a victim in fact has come forward as an adult and requested that allegations not be made public. They might say, "Look, I'm married now. I have a family. My life is coming together. I don't want the media coming to my house. I don't want my children bothered. I don't want the publicity." The Church respects that confidentiality and is in a dilemma about turning over lists of priests and their victims. And the fact also is that payments to the victims were not always hush money as much as attempts to help them pay for therapy and rebuild their lives. Frequently the amounts were kept secret at the request of the insurance companies themselves, which also often preferred to settle out of court because the legal fees were so high whether they won or not.

Zero tolerance limitations

Fifth, although there is the popular cry for a zero tolerance policy, it does have its limitations and provokes a certain amount of unfairness if not, like all zero tolerance policies, a certain amount of lunacy. One thinks of the sixteen year old in Texas who was helping his grandmother move. In the course of moving her, one of her kitchen knives accidentally fell out of the box into the back of his pickup truck. He unknowingly carried the knife in the truck to school the next day where someone spotted it. Under the school's zero tolerance policy he was expelled. An eight-year-old boy from Arkansas was suspended for three days after pointing a breaded chicken finger at a teacher and saying "Pow, pow, pow." Under the zero tolerance policy students have been punished for giving mints to classmates, possessing nail clippers, and taking a plastic ax to a Halloween party.

So it is no surprise that such a policy would be less than perfect in cases of alleged priest abuse. This policy, which has the fingerprints of lawyers all over it, means that an accused priest is defrocked and immediately forfeits clerical life. Suppose, for example, that twenty-five years ago a good priest, having had a little too much to drink at a family party, bends over and kisses a twelve-year-old girl on the cheek and touches her breast. The next day, with a clearer head, he is embarrassed and utterly mortified. He's never done anything like that before and certainly won't do it again. It was a moment of weakness.

Suppose the girl, now a grown woman, has a "recovered memory" of the incident and brings an allegation of sexual abuse. Is this priest, caught in the zero tolerance policy, to be summarily put in the same category as a priest who repeatedly sodomized an eight-year-old boy and dismissed? Some, especially those who still feel outrage, would think he should. Others are more willing to see this as a one-time human failing of a good person and, with a watchful eye, let it go. Or think of a priest who did abuse a minor twenty-five or thirty years ago (the common time slot on all these accusations), who has repented, taken a ministry where others are safe, has done fine work, and now finds his life shattered by mandatory exposure.

The fact is that some sexual abusers are quite responsive to treatment. True pedophiles who prey on pre-pubescent children are probably unable to be treated successfully. But most abusers, as we shall see in the next chapter, are not pedophiles but ephebophiles, that is, people who prey on post-pubescent minors or adolescents. As Stephen Rossetti, who is a psychologist and a consultant to the bishops, writes:

> Fortunately, real pedophiles are the exception among adults who sexually abuse minors. Most abusers are not pedophiles. Most abuse post-pubescent minors and, all things being equal, are much more amenable to treatment. While both pedophiles and those who molest post-pubescent minors have committed a heinous crime, it would be an error to apply exactly the same remedy to them all. With treatment and supervision, many adults who molest adolescents can go on to live productive lives. But prudence would still dictate that these adults should be supervised whenever interacting with adolescents....Fred Berlin, M.D., an international expert on the treatment of child abusers, reported a relapse rate of only 2.9 per-

cent over a five- to six-year period among 173 lay abusers who were treatment-compliant. (*America,* April 22, 2002)

An article in the *New York Times* (April 21) focuses on a treatment center in Jemez Springs, New Mexico. Note that this center has been operating for almost twenty years. (Yes, the bishops were getting their act together around that time.) The article points out what we have been saying all along and what statistics consistently show: that the abusive priests who go there are seldom true pedophiles. Rather they are homosexual abusers of adolescent boys. And once more, while some may have abused again, the fact is that most priests treated there have altered their behavior and have gone back to rebuild their lives safely as laymen or priests. Noting again that the victims were adolescent boys and that this finding is supported by other studies and the observations of experts, the article adds this sentence: "It is significant, scientists said, because adults who become sexually involved with adolescents are considered more amenable to treatment than pedophiles."

The parallels to alcoholism

At this point, it is entirely apt, I think, to draw parallels between alcoholism and sexual abuse. As we shall mention again later, alcoholism is considered not curable but treatable. Ephebophilia is, at the present state of our understanding, also considered the same way. If you are an alcoholic or know one, you know there is a vast distinction between a chronic abusing alcoholic and a "dry" one. We do not apply a zero tolerance rule to them indiscriminately. We imprison the one and accept the other.

Yes, of course, any alcoholic may revert and drink and drive and kill someone. But if they remain dry, go to their weekly AA meeting, and keep in touch with their sponsor, we don't take their driver's license away or throw them out of the house or club or job. Yes, at one time they did indeed abuse alcohol and did harm others, but we are perfectly aware that, if there is not a cure, there is rehabilitation and they give every sign of being rehabilitated. The reason we know that is that you and I have wonderful alcoholic friends who have been dry and responsible for many, many years.

The question is, should it be any different for priest sexual abusers? Yes, throw the chronic, serial abusers into jail and toss away the key. But what about those priests who have in fact rehabilitated themselves? Yes, like the alcoholic, there is always the possibility that they may revert, but they go to their weekly meetings with the therapist and keep in touch with their mentors. They have been "dry" for many years. Do we throw their license away? Expose them?

I think this was what the cardinals were trying to come to terms with at the meeting in Rome when, much to most people's dismay, they stopped short of endorsing a "one-strike-you're-out" or zero tolerance policy. They made a distinction between "serial" and "notorious" abusers and those who were not, declaring that the former should be dismissed while the latter might be dealt with on an individual basis to see if they're safe and functional. These latter cases might be less clear cut and it would have to be determined on a one-to-one basis whether such a priest could be rehabilitated or at least no longer considered a threat to children.

The cardinals were sympathetically trying to make the reformed alcoholic equal to a reformed abuser. As I said, this distinction, in the current climate, brought immediate negative reaction. And perhaps that's understandable, given the need at this moment for a strong gesture. In any case, the truth is that a zero tolerance policy, while still debated, is actually much more in favor with some of the cardinals and bishops than not, and my guess is that at the June meeting all of the bishops will adopt it as a national policy. One thing is for sure: across the board, the Catholic people want a zero tolerance policy, and even if treatment is effective, the consensus is that rehabilitated priests can function as good human beings elsewhere, but not as priests.

Still, if one-strike-you're-out prevails the question remains, out where? The answer is out there—on the outside—untreated and unmonitored. If you defrock priests and kick them out, who's going to be watching them? You simply dump them out on the street to be a danger to minors. On the other hand, if child abuse, like alcoholism, is not curable (at least in current thought) but can be contained under guarded circumstances, ought not a priest in therapy be given a chance to work in areas apart from children?

As Thomas Plante, author of *Bless Me, Father for I Have Sinned,* put it, "If you're making jam in some Midwestern monastery, you're not going to be offending." Just as you wouldn't let an alcoholic tend bar but offer him creative work elsewhere, so such priests would not be around children or even wear a Roman collar, but they could still minister and help others. This seems more in keeping with the gospel. Still, others do not agree. They feel, especially right now, that any abuser priest in any kind of Church position gives a wrong signal.

Others contend that a zero tolerance policy does not allow for due process and in summarily handing over suspect priests to prosecutors, bishops who are running scared are trampling on the rights of priests. Priests, even with a whiff of scandal, are punished. As we said, some innocent priests have been falsely swept up in the purge. And now their reputations are in ruin. Is this just, they ask? At least might not a diocese establish an advocate to handle such accusations, to begin a due process that assumes innocence first?

Jail or treatment?

Sixth, there is this question: sexually abusing clergy should be dismissed and punished, but should they be turned over to the criminal justice system? There is compassionate hesitation here, for today's conventional wisdom, as we have noted above, is that if pedophilia, like alcoholism, is incurable it is also, like alcoholism, treatable. And there are centers that do treat sexual abusers. Over the years, obviously, such centers have shifted approaches. Early on, they focused on the physical. They often recommended castration or a lobotomy.

Today the focus is on a multi-level approach of behavioral adjustment, psychological techniques, small group dynamics, and medication. As a result, some sex offenders, as we have noted above, are effectively treated. They may have minimal relapses, which often do not involve physical contact. While such priests may not be returned to ministry, society is generally safe from them and they can live productive lives, as many of my alcoholic friends do. The point is that to send people with sexual disorders to prison is both ineffective and inhumane. The point also is that, if the Church forces a man to leave the ministry, it has done nothing to put in place the necessary treatment and supervision he needs.

Finally, to round out our perspective, the issue of forgiveness also nags. This is a priest who sinned. He sinned seventy times seven. You hate the sin, but, again, this is your brother and you have to love him. And forgive. One recalls the scene from John Grisham's book, *The Testament*, where he describes a scene in which Nate, the alcoholic attorney, is in church:

> The young man in the pulpit was praying, his eyes clenched tightly, his arms waving gently upward. Nate closed his eyes too, and called God's name. God was waiting.
>
> With both hands, he clenched the back of the pew front of him. He repeated the list, mumbling every weakness and flaw and affliction and evil that plagued him. He confessed them all. In one long glorious acknowledgment of failure, he laid himself bare before God. He held nothing back. He unloaded enough burdens to crush any three men, and when he finally finished Nate had tears in his eyes. "I'm sorry," he whispered to God. "Please help me."
>
> As quickly as the fever had left his body he felt baggage leave his soul. With one gentle brush of the hand, his slate had been wiped clean He breathed a sigh of relief, but his pulse was racing. He heard the guitar again. He opened his eyes and wiped his cheeks. Instead of seeing the young man in the pulpit Nate saw the face of Christ, in agony and pain dying on the cross. Dying for him. (New York: Doubleday, 1999).

Christ did indeed die for Nate—and for the perpetrators too. Priests look for inspiration to the example of their brother priest, Father Jim Carney, a missionary in Honduras, who prayed for his murderers before they threw him out of a helicopter to his death below. They try to imitate him. Not always successfully. The Catholic clergy are conflicted but they are hopeful. And all of us know, clergy and laity, that not all of the apostles were perfect: three slept, two jockeyed for first place, one denied Jesus, one doubted, and the one betrayed him. Six out of twelve isn't great odds. By every accounting the Church should never have gotten off the ground given the sinful performance of the apostles. But the Church did get off the ground and the repentant, second-chance apostles proved their sincerity by laying down their lives for the gospel.

I must admit that all this is a hard sell. "Treatment," "forgiveness"—they sound good, but people are very angry. They don't want to hear about these things. That's understandable. But, down the road, no matter how far down, healing will have to include both.

This has been a difficult chapter. But all I ask is that you ponder the issues from a broad perspective and do not let the media form your head and heart. The situation of clergy sexual abuser is indeed horrendous, but to deal with it we need more than headlines and emotional reactions. We need to see what we did wrong in order to correct it. We also need to see what we did right in order to reinforce it.

Questions for Discussion

1. When you were growing up, did you experience or hear about clergy who molested others?

2. Priests, like teachers, scoutmasters, and others who work with children are afraid to befriend or hug a child. How do you feel about this?

3. The prosecutors want lists of names of any priest who has ever been accused. The diocese will give the names but want confidentiality lest a good name be vilified. What do you think?

4. Should erring priests be dismissed, sent to jail, or sent for treatment?

5. Do you favor a one-strike-you're-out policy? Do you think that sexual abusers, like alcohol abusers, can be rehabilitated?

6. Do you find it hard to forgive those who commit sexual abuse with children? Do you feel differently if the situation involves teenagers?

FIVE

Precision

When Jesus stepped out of the boat, immediately a man out of the tombs with an unclean spirit met him...and he shouted at the top of his voice, "What have you to do with me, Jesus...." Then Jesus asked him, "What is your name?" He replied, "My name is Legion for we are many." —Mk 5:2–9

You may have noticed that all along I have assiduously avoided using the term so dear to the news media: pedophile. The media loves to headline every breathless article or television special under the bright banner of "Pedophile Priests." That only perpetuates common misconceptions. This is why some precision is in order.

Pedophilia is a sexual preference for and activity with pre-pubescent children. Ephebophilia, as we noted in the last chapter, is a sexual preference for and activity with pubescent children; in other words, adolescents. The distinction is crucial, for the statistical fact is that most adult sexual abusers, clergy and non-clergy alike, abuse adolescents. It doesn't make the crime less horrible but it does lessen the impact a great deal.

If you banter about the issue of priest pedophiles without qualification, you conjure up dirty old men abusing six or seven year olds. This happens. But far more frequent is the abuse of teenagers, all of whom are victims but not quite in the same way. For one thing, most sexual abuse cases involve older teenagers above the legal age of consent. They can cooperate to a degree. They can flee or fight. They can more readily speak up. Of course, let me hasten to add that, intimidated by the aura of such an authority figure, none of this is likely. But, still, there is a degree of autonomy that is not present with the little child.

As Philip Jenkins, author of *Pedophiles and Priests*, says, "I don't want to excuse the behavior. Having sex with a sixteen- or seventeen-year-old boy or girl may be phenomenally stupid and wrong in many ways—immoral, sinful, and an abuse of authority—but it's very different from pedophilia, which is the exploitation of prepubescent children. In most of these cases with older teenagers, there is some degree of consent and in most jurisdictions they're legal." (The age of consent is seventeen in New York and sixteen in many other places. In the Netherlands it's twelve and some gay groups, like the North American Man-Boy Love Association (NAMBLA), are lobbying to get the age even lower.) By using such a term as "sexual abusers" we avoid lumping together, as does the media, the pedophile who preys on tiny children and ephebophiles who prey on adolescents.

(As an afterthought concerning the zero tolerance policy, we might note Dr. Jenkins' distinctions: "If you have a pedophile, the behavior is likely to be deeply obsessive and very hard to cure. The Church is taking a suicidal risk in sending a pedophile to a parish. But when it's someone who had sex with an older teenager, then with treatment and proper supervision and restrictions, the priest might well not cause further problems.")

What we're dealing with, then, when we speak about clergy sexual abuse, is not properly pedophilia, the abuse of prepubescent children, but mostly ephebophilia, the abuse of teenagers, mostly boys. In fact, it is estimated that ninety percent of the victims of Catholic clergy sexual abuse are teenage boys.

Increasing understanding

What do we know about pedophilia (to stick with that term for the sake of discussion)? Not much. Our knowledge is still far from complete even though advances have been made. For one thing, the condition of pedophilia does not seem to be an inherited state although there is some research that might suggest biological roots. The condition does seem to be more a learned behavior with an addictive quality, and it seems to develop at a young age.

In the ancient shadows and twilight
Where childhood has strayed
The world's great sorrows were born
And its heroes were made.
In the lost childhood of Judas
Christ was betrayed.

("Germinal," by "A.E.")

Moreover, pedophiles often become quite aware of their tendencies when quite young, certainly around adolescence. Usually, it takes a while for them to act on these tendencies. One therapist said that most priests he has counseled began to act on their attractions by the time they were in their early to mid-twenties.

Often the behavior of pedophiles is connected with the pedophile's own victimization at the hands of another, although not all abused children become pedophiles. And what causes it in those who have not been abused is not known. In any case, one thing is sure: pedophiles don't choose to be that way. Those who work with child abusers often notice the lack of any moral sense or feelings of remorse and guilt for what they have done. They don't seem to be in any moral torment for their behaviors. They have to be brought to a point of realization of the immorality of what they have done.

Pedophiles at any age are not visibly distinguishable from other people. You can't tell who they are by looking at them. There don't seem to be any common features in terms of personality or temperament, whether they're introverts or extroverts, or their level of intelligence. Alcohol or drugs do not figure in the equation except, of course, that these may lower inhibitions. Pedophiles may have reasonably healthy relationships with other adults. They can even have a normal sex life with their spouses. But they're also dealing with the strong attraction to children.

In short, the only invisible common element is the difficulty pedophiles have in dealing with their sexual needs in a constructive fashion. There's really no clue that someone is going to be a risk outside of noticing that he or she is spending an unusual amount of time with children, unchaperoned. Most abusers are male although, as we shall see later, abuse by females is more common than is admitted.

Pedophiles' strong attraction to children may start off innocently enough. Clergy, Boy Scout leaders, social workers, teachers all have a positive non-sexual relationship with children. For the pedophiles among them, however, this may lead to unwanted sexual activity, and often we read of such people with access to children being charged with abuse. At times, the cravings are so strong that abusers convince themselves that what they're doing isn't harmful. Only in hindsight, under treatment, do they realize the full horror of betrayal.

In any case, there is usually a kind of evolution leading up to the abuse. Seldom is there a conscious plot to seduce a child. The pedophile, almost always known to the victim (usually a parent, stepparent, relative, friend) usually has a genuine affection for the child and is interested in him in a positive way. But then such contacts, familiarity, and trust give way to temptation and finally to abuse. In other words, the abuse is at the end term of weeks and even months, progressing from an interested non-sexual relationship to a sexual one.

The bishops' dilemma

None of this was known thirty or forty years ago when most of the current cases that have surfaced happened. None of us reading this page had ever heard the words pedophile or ephebophilia. None of us had the limited knowledge we have today about child abuse or even how common it was. This is important to remember for this general ignorance included the bishops. When sexual abuse cases came to their attention the bishops automatically, because of their training, bracketed them in therapeutic and moral categories. The experts had told them that sex cases were like alcoholism and were treatable.

Consequently, you just don't blame people for having a disease, much less throw them out. This was not radical sin for which you would dismiss someone. This was an illness you treated. You work them back into the community when they're cured. Then, too, remember, there was grace. The heart of Christianity says that there are no irredeemable sinners. It just didn't fit Christian moral consciousness that a person would be incurable. Therapy, a good retreat, confession, a prayer life, should do the trick. If one had strong moral resolve, he would be able to return to work. Finally, the whole case was kept secret because one didn't really want to parade one's sinfulness before the world.

This was the context for everyone at that time, even for bishops. So, it worked like this. If the bishop were apprised of an alleged case of sexual abuse, he would call in the offending priest. If it were established that the priest was at fault he would be sent to a center for treatment. The doctors and psychiatrists there, say, would pronounce the man fit to go back and he would be reassigned. The medical community, as we said, did not understand fully the nature of the disease. They admit that today. So the most common scenario was that the bishop took them at their word and reassigned the man. The victim was given some compensation and as often as not, as we mentioned previously, insisted that their name never be surfaced since they were so embarrassed.

No one wants to deny that there were gross cases of negligence and cover-ups by some bishops but for the most part, the average bishop, like the average anyone else in those days, followed the advice of the "experts." Things were not as sinister and conspiratorial as the press makes them out to be and, to that extent, we simply do not know how widespread any cover-ups have been. Where even good bishops were at fault, however, and seriously so, was that, as the understanding of pedophilia increased and, as the exposure of so many cases began to surface in the mid-eighties, they should have been more alert, more sensitive, and more active. They should have been more persistent in enforcing the principles they had begun to use in the mid- 1990s. In the past fifteen to twenty years there has been too much handwriting on the wall to ignore. Those who did are now paying the price.

Questions for Discussion

1. The distinction between pedophilia and ephebophilia is important. Discuss.

2. The bishops, during the time when many abuses occurred, followed the advice of the experts who themselves knew little enough about the basis of child molestation. Do you think they acted rightly?

SIX

Perception

A voice was heard in Ramah, wailing and loud lamentation,
Rachel weeping for her children; she refused to be consoled.

—Mt 2:18

There is a dangerous distraction in the unrelenting focus on abusive priests. The danger lies in exposing, prosecuting, and ultimately "cleansing" the Church. Once the Church is properly humbled, then the task is done, the problem is solved. But Catholic clergy sexual abuse, as horrific as it is, is but a subdivision of a much larger and pervasive problem of child victimization.

We have pointed out, for example, that the rate of abuse in the Catholic Church is no higher than among other clergy and other professions. I was reminded of this when, before writing this chapter, there appeared in the papers, buried on page eight or so, the account of a teacher accused of sexually molesting five girls. Tales of teachers, scout leaders, and coaches abusing students are standard fare and cumulatively over the years add up to considerable numbers. I have before me a website page from Education Week listing the titles of a six-month-long project that looked into schoolteacher and school employees' abuse of children. Some of the titles are instructive: "At One California School a Never-ending Nightmare," "Cost is High When Schools Ignore Abuse," "In Youth's Tender Emotions, Abusers Find Easy Pickings." All the surveys, which were done in 1998, uncover a significant amount of teacher-student sexual abuse. Yet most teachers are moral.

Years ago there was a big hubbub over psychiatrists having sexual affairs with their patients, some of them justifying such affairs as therapy. There is the constant disagreement over college and university professors having sex with their students, as some justify consensual relationships with those of legal age.

There is a professional writer by the name of Dee Ann Miller who writes on sexual abuse by Protestant clergy, and she has formed a huge network of women abused by their ministers or who had affairs with them. (One readily thinks of the Rev. Martin Luther King, Jr., the Rev. Jesse Jackson, and the TV evangelists Jimmy Swaggart and Jim Bakker). She points to a survey published in the 1993 edition of *The Journal of Pastoral Care* which revealed that fourteen percent of Baptist ministers surveyed admitted to "engagement in sexual behavior which was judged by the individual pastors to be inappropriate for a minister." She is appalled at the stonewalling and always asks when she gives her lectures, "Why do professional ministers and laity collude to recycle violent ministers from one congregation to another in secrecy?" She too speaks of errant ministers who received counseling and, given a clean bill of mental health, were returned to minister in another church.

Other denominations

A study in 1990 by the Park Ridge Center for the Study of Health, Faith, and Ethics found that ten percent of the nation's ministers had admitted having an affair with members of their congregation. About twenty-five percent said they had had some sexual contact with a parishioner. Prominent, high-echelon Protestants who have been accused of sexual misconduct include Lutheran Bishop Lowell Mays and the Rev. James Armstrong, past president of the National Council of Churches. These abuses usually deal with adult women but the point is that sexual abuse among other clergy besides Catholics exists.

In 1992, for example, in a case that received national attention, a Colorado jury awarded more than a million dollars to a woman who had been abused by an Episcopal priest and held the local diocese liable for the damages. In February of this year (2002) a jury ordered a former Lutheran pastor to pay damages to a woman with whom he had sexual relations; but here the jury did not hold the national Church liable. That very same month a Maryland Episcopal priest, Kenneth Behrel, was found guilty of abusing a fourteen-year-old boy in the 1980s. A Lutheran pastor from Texas, Gerard Thomas, Jr., is facing charges of abusing a teenage boy. His Lutheran officials are also charged because they, knowing his record, passed him on to different parishes.

One lawyer estimates that she has handled fifty cases of clerical abuse in the past twenty years, involving the Methodist Church, the Episcopal Church, the Church of Christ, and the Church of the Nazarene. One thinks of the huge scandal in March of 2002 concerning Howard Nevison, a famous Jewish cantor at New York's most prestigious synagogue, Temple Emanu-El in Manhattan, who was accused of molesting his young nephew. A recent book by Gary Schoener, a clinical psychologist and authority on sex abuse, is titled *Sexual Abuse by Rabbis*. The head of the Mormon Church, at its seventy-second semi-annual general conference in April of 2002, acknowledged child sexual abuse within his own church. And all of these churches stonewall. As Jeffrey Anderson, one of the nation's leading authorities on the subject of clergy misconduct says, "It's hard to say that any church has been a model in this area. Most religious groups have reacted with denial at some point."

Female abusers

Let's not forget that there are women sexual abusers. This very notion unsettles us. We know men abuse and indeed, they constitute the majority of abusers. But there are a significant number of women who sexually abuse others, although we seldom hear about them. The accepted wisdom is that men are perpetrators; men cannot be victims. Women are victims; women cannot be perpetrators. Men rape; women do not. But, as Robert J. Shoop, an expert on sexual harassment prevention at Kansas State University has put it, "Society is being confronted by the fact that both men and women can behave inappropriately, and that young boys are just as vulnerable to abuse as young girls." A while back a show called *Panorama*, on Britain's BBC, focused on women who sexually abuse children and on domestic violence by women. A 1996 study found that women were responsible for twenty percent of child sexual abuse. Dr. David Thornton, an international expert on child abuse, says that America is just starting to accept the fact that women commit sex crimes as well as men.

Most of us know about the married teacher in New England who molested a boy and had him kill her husband. What we don't hear about is how widespread such female molestation is and how it is treated with much more sympathy than male molestation. The trouble is that it is often hushed up, and women who are involved with male students are simply treated less harshly.

Here is a case in point. MenWeb, a web site on men's issues, posted a story from the Seattle *Times* by columnist Terry McDermott. In his column he contrasted two cases of child molestation and how his paper handled them. One story was about Mark Billie, forty-two years old, married, and the father of two children, who had sex with a fifteen-year-old girl, a former student of his. Another was about a female teacher, Ms. Letourneau, who had an affair with a thirteen-year-old boy and had a child by him. The paper's attitude towards each story couldn't have been more different. The paper described Ms. Letourneau as appearing "in an aquamarine sweater, black pleated skirt, and her hair pinned up with soft tendrils." Other papers described her as blond and attractive. By contrast there was no physical description given of Mr. Billie at all, although his photograph showed him to be tall and handsome. The captions beneath their photographs identified him as "convicted child rapist, Mark Billie" and her as "a former teacher." It's this sort of thing that points up both the inequity of treatment and the silence about the problem with male sexual abusers and female sexual abusers.

Here is a statistic: of the nearly 250 cases of alleged sexual misconduct between staff and students reviewed by *Education Week*, forty-three of them, or nearly one in five, involved female employees. In five of those cases the victims were girls; the rest were boys in middle school or high school, ranging in age from eleven to seventeen.

Boys, it might be noted, suffer from cultural expectations. If a girl is abused, it is alarming. On the other hand, if a female abuses a boy, the response might be, "Aren't you lucky!" Or the episode is often looked upon as a rite of initiation into sex and a feeling that a boy is fortunate to be initiated so young. Moreover, as one counselor said, because boys often freely agree to sex with a woman such as a teacher, women often have trouble knowing that they are doing any harm. They think they're giving the kid a huge gift. The trouble is, as another counselor put it, "A fifteen-year-old girl having sex with a thirty-year-old man would be recognized pretty clearly as sexual abuse. Reverse the gender and many people have a more difficult time calling that sexual abuse."

The wider picture

Sadly, the sexual abuse of children worldwide is much larger than we have ever thought. It is estimated by the American Medical Association that two-thirds of sexual assaults, whether on adults or minors, are never reported. The sexual abuse of boys, so often buried and underestimated, is much higher than we ever thought. Boys are raped at an alarming rate. The standard study on human sexuality shows that seventeen percent of women and twelve percent of men report that they were abused before they reached puberty, and often repeatedly. Girls stood a risk of being abused by adult men and adolescent males while boys stood a greater risk from adolescent women.

Estimates from the experts range from 300,000 to 400,000 reported cases of abuse a year, the vast majority of them perpetrated by family members. There is worldwide trafficking in women and children who are used as servants and sex slaves. It is also estimated that every year, some 50,000 of them are imported to the United States. Planeloads of men travel to places like Thailand to find boys. The problem is enormous.

The reason for all this distasteful cataloguing is to point up what was said at the beginning of this chapter: the rate of sexual abuse among Catholic clergy is not an epidemic, as the media would lead us to believe, and the number of incidents is not unique. The rate of Catholic clergy abuse falls into the same percentages as abuse by other professionals and clergy and the general public. It's just that accusations of sexual abuse by Catholic clergy tend to get written up far more often than sexual abuse in other churches because of three reasons.

The first reason is a longstanding bias against the Church; there is no doubt that a good deal of Catholic bashing exists here. This bias also leads to a serious omission by the media, namely, as we have seen, the work that the bishops have already done. During the past fifteen years, they have, in fact, put in place measures to prevent clerical sexual abuse. In general, their efforts have been very effective. The Boston scandal did not suddenly expose a wholly unaddressed problem. The bishops are being judged by how they got it wrong and not how they got it right.

The second reason is that, while the Catholic Church does not have more sexual abusers than other institutions, it also doesn't have a system of open accountability. There is no real transparency in the way the system works. This is a fatal flaw that leads to all kind of curiosity, rumor, and speculation by the press.

But there is also a final reason. The Catholic Church is an easier, more definable corporate target than other denominations because of its hierarchical, top-down structure. Technically speaking, the priest is accountable to the bishop—not to the people—who in turn is accountable to the pope. This makes the pope responsible for the bishop and the bishop responsible for the priest. This whole system makes it easier to prove institutional irresponsibility in cases of child sexual abuse, especially when the institution moves a proven predator around. That's why lawyers are suing dioceses and even the Vatican: the Church's hierarchical administrative structure makes it far easier to pursue a case against it and win a substantial settlement.

Also, we might mention that an added incentive to suing the Church here in the United States is that this country, unlike other countries, has an adversary system along with peculiar laws that call for enormous sums of money to be paid out for litigation and punitive damages. In other words, in this country the litigation and recovery system is enormously lucrative. To give just two examples: if you have an accident in Canada and lose a limb you can collect several hundred thousand dollars. In the U.S., for the same accident, you can collect up to several million dollars. In Britain a judge awarded some $60,000 to thirteen plaintiffs who were sexually abused. In contrast, in Texas, a jury ordered the diocese of Dallas to pay $120,000,000 to eleven plaintiffs. Lawyers here can receive as much as forty percent of the settlement so a lawyer who sues, say, for $100,000,000 on behalf of 600 clients will pocket $40,000,000 and the remainder will be divided up among the others.

Such news, of course, is not put forward to make excuses or make any of us feel better. There is no attempt to relieve any of us of our anguish and shame. This is no warrant not to commiserate deeply with the victims. These citations are meant rather to put things into perspective so that we can deal not only with abusive Catholic clergy, but also with all those in our society who prey on children. Who knows: maybe someday, a chastened Church, like a reformed alcoholic, can take the lead in educating people as to the problem and provide support groups.

Questions for Discussion

1. The sexual abuse by Catholic clergy is but a small, though evil, percentage of child molestation cases. Discuss.

2. The vast majority of child molestation cases, estimated at some 400,000 annually, are perpetrated by family members, mostly parents, siblings, relatives. Many are never reported. Discuss.

3. Are you surprised to find that females also molest children?

4. Should the Church, humbled, lead the way in education, about sexual abuse, and provide support groups for victims?

SEVEN

The Gay Connection

Do not ordain anyone hastily. —1 Tim 5:22

If you go back over the previous pages, one fact stands out glaringly: those abused are largely boys. The priests, the bishops, are almost always abusing teenage boys—not their secretary or their secretary's daughters. Almost every newly revealed victim tearfully appearing on television is a male. Some clinicians report that ninety percent of priests' sexual victims are male. The inevitable and undeniable conclusion is that most of the clerical perpetrators are homosexual. Philip Jenkins, writing in the *Wall Street Journal* (March 26, 2002) says:

> Most priests of gay orientation probably succeeded in keeping their vows of chastity, but enough misbehaved to account for the majority of cases that have come to light in recent months. Virtually all of these cases involve sex between men and older teenagers rather than pedophilia. If we are looking for a one-word description of most of the acts, we should properly be speaking of "homosexuality."

This raises a hotly debated issue: are homosexuals by nature predators, and is the issue of clergy abuse mainly a homosexual issue? Get rid of the gays and you get rid of the problem? Or is it that gays are no more likely to be sexual predators than straights and that it's only just a startling coincidence that the vast majority of clerical abusers of teenage boys are gay?

Those on the "gays are the problem" side include most Catholics on the right, including the Vatican's chief spokesman, Dr. Joaquin Navarro-Valls. He went so far as to declare that gay men should not be ordained; indeed, he stated that gay men *cannot* be validly ordained because, he said, it's like a gay man marrying a woman who is unaware of his orientation. Just as such a marriage would be invalid so would an ordination. Furthermore, he added, if a gay man were ordained, all his acts would be invalid. All of which has led A.W. Richard Sipe, a psychotherapist who has worked extensively on clerical sexual abuse, to remark wryly that throwing homosexual priests out of the priesthood would decimate an already shrinking priesthood—not to mention that a third of the world's bishops would have to resign. And if all those sacraments celebrated by a gay priest were declared invalid, who knows how many millions of baptisms and marriages would be null and void!

The doctor's remarks, as expected, brought angry responses. Andrew Sullivan, a sexually active homosexual Catholic columnist, shot back that homosexual priests should not be made the scapegoats. "Rather than tackle its own culpability for protecting child molesters," he wrote, "the Vatican decided to use the ancient slur of associating pedophiles with homosexuals to deflect the blame, at the same time smearing the many excellent, holy, and dedicated gay priests."

Those on the "gays are *not* the problem" side include Catholics on the left, who point to another undeniable factor: that many priests—estimates vary from fifty percent to sixty percent—are gay, and so it's a question of mathematics. That is, if there is going to be child abuse, that child will be male because the large pool of gay priests will predict it. Think of it this way: there is no surprise at excessive and destructive drinking and drunkenness at the union hall if seventy-five percent of their members are alcoholics. There is no reason, then, claims this group of defenders, to believe that homosexuality of itself automatically breeds sexual abusers or that the numbers of them who do abuse are any different from heterosexual males in general. It would rather seem that, if there is going to be sexual abuse by priests, the target of that abuse would be boys. This reflects not any intrinsic connection to homosexuality, but a statistic: clerical abusers happen to be largely gay because there are so many of them in the priesthood.

And there are so many of them, the defenders say, because if you're going to restrict the pool to celibate males then you're naturally going to draw a disproportionate number of homosexual men who don't want to get married anyway. A small percentage of these men are exceedingly sexually immature males who turn out to be the abusers. They argue, then, that the real culprit is not homosexuality but celibacy.

Nevertheless, there is no getting around the fact that many of the abusers are indeed homosexual, and this was noted at the meeting the pope called in April of 2002. In my view, what seemed to emerge from that meeting—although no one would say it out loud—is a quota system. That is, bishops will be wary of ordaining too many homosexual men. They will reject most and keep only those whom they are morally sure will live a celibate life. Others, like Cardinal Bevilacqua of Philadelphia, take a more extreme view. He has said outright that he won't ordain anyone who is homosexual regardless of how faithful he is.

Well, my comment is that there go two of the most well-known and effective priests in our country: the late spiritual writer, Henri Nouwen, whose books have had such a profound impact on millions of readers; and Father Mychal Judge, who gave his life so heroically at Ground Zero on September 11, 2001.

Anyway, Catholics seem divided on the issue. Gay Catholics feel that they are being unfairly targeted, and point out that there is no credible data to say that homosexuals are more likely than heterosexuals to molest children. Whatever their position, the reason for the bishops' wariness is not necessarily homophobic. The reason is that not only are so many perpetrators homosexual but also that statistically there are so many homosexuals who are priests—at least enough to cause some heterosexual men to leave the priesthood and seminaries and others not to join. The bishops are aiming for balance.

The record

The presence of so many gay priests has not gone unnoticed in the past. As early as 1987, Richard McBrien, writing in a national Catholic magazine, brought up the issue. Two years later, in a national Catholic newspaper, Andrew Greeley wrote about "lavender rectories." He wrote, "Blatantly active homosexual priests are appointed, transferred, and promoted....National networks of active homosexual priests (many of them Church administrators) are tolerated. Pedophiles are reassigned."

One seminary was known as the "pink palace." Peter McDonough and Eugene Bianchi, in their new book on the Jesuits which tracks the rise and fall of the order, speak of "the gaying and graying of the Jesuits." They reveal that so much of a gay subculture flourishes in this order that many heterosexual Jesuits were forced to leave, and that Jesuits by the dozens were suffering from AIDS.

Once more, we see the destructiveness of secrecy. The bishops obviously knew about the large presence of homosexual seminarians and priests, and simply looked the other way or did not deal with it. In the 1980s, for example, when Richard Schoenherr did his survey of priests on behalf of the bishops he was not allowed to pursue the issue of sexual orientation. He wrote, "While it has been a concern for some time to many U.S. Catholics, the U.S. bishops have adamantly refused to gather information on the sexual inclination of priests."

A.W. Richard Sipe started to gather data on priests from 1960 to 1985 and noted how the numbers of homosexual priests increased over the three decades. He reported that by 1985 about one-fifth of all American priests had "some homosexual orientation," and he predicted that, if the trend continued, by the year 2012, more than half of the American clergy would be gay.

In June of 1995, a dozen American bishops issued a joint protest against their own organization, the National Conference of Catholic Bishops (NCCB), because of their lack of candor in coming to terms with those well-founded rumors about the high percentage of gay seminarians and priests. They were incensed that the subject could not even be openly discussed or talked about;

there was suppression and denial all the way around. The fact is that the bishops knew not just that there were homosexuals in the priesthood, which in itself might not be a problem, but that many homosexual priests were sexually active; that, in fact, they were "organized." Some of the bishops themselves were gay, of course, but had they reined in the problem at that time, we would not have the scandal now.

The findings

In the year 2000, Donald Cozzens, a respected seminary rector, professor of pastoral studies, and vicar for priests, wrote a book called *The Changing Face of the Priesthood*, a careful, balanced book that openly revealed the extent of the problem of gays in the priesthood. This book, widely publicized and reviewed, sent shockwaves throughout the Church and gleaned considerable public interest. The biggest revelation in this book (backed up by subsequent studies) is that there is a significantly higher percentage of homosexual priests and seminarians than there are in society at large. We don't know exact numbers, but those in seminaries and those who have been around a while all speak of the disproportionate number of gay men in the priesthood and seminaries. One report showed that

Catholic seminarians score highest on the femininity scale of the MMPI...these seminarians felt insecure and inferior. This insecurity seemed to be partly due to the anxiety of trying to live out these "feminine" traits in a masculinized and patriarchal culture.... Frank Kobler, who investigated screening tests for applicants to the religious life, found that his sample of 323 minor seminarians "had profiles that resembled those for females in the general population." Solid psychological evidence now supports an old suspicion: boys and young men with a feminine perception of themselves tended to be attracted to a vocation....One survey of priests in 1984 revealed that only two out of every ten priests actually saw themselves as masculine, while four out of ten admitted to a strong feminine identification. (William D. Perri, *A Radical Challenge for the Priesthood Today*, Twenty-Third Publications)

An NBC report on celibacy found that "anywhere from twenty-three to fifty-eight percent" of the Catholic clergy have a homosexual orientation. Other studies indicate that half of the clergy population has a homosexual orientation; the percentage of gay priests in religious congregations appears to be even higher. (As expected, not far from the question of the number of gay priests is the issue of AIDS. In spite of recent publicity on the issue, it remains, for the official Church, a secret and closed topic. Nevertheless, the fact that some priests have died from this disease can be documented.)

The columnist who calls him self "Pastor Ignotus" in the *Tablet*, Britain's Catholic periodical, noted:

> Equally disturbing is the tendency of bishops to overlook the fact that a disproportionate number of homosexuals are being recruited into our seminaries. I know of one seminary where, two years ago, sixty percent of the students identified themselves as "gay," twenty percent were confused about their sexual identity, and only twenty percent considered themselves heterosexual. I have no objections whatsoever to welcoming homosexuals into the priesthood. I know some excellent priests who are homosexual and that has never been a problem in their ministry. But there would be cause for concern if, in order to maintain the status quo, the Catholic priesthood was allowed to become primarily a "gay" option.

Why gays are attracted to the priesthood is open to much speculation. There are those in the past (the perpetrators are largely from the 1950s and '60s) who, before homosexuality went mainstream as it is today, thought that their confused sense of male identity might find some protection and control in the priesthood. They could exchange their anguished identity as an outsider for a respected identity as an insider. Or they could find a legitimate and honorable way to stay unmarried, enjoy the company of fellow male priests, and receive respect from the public. Or they knew their work would bring them in close contact with women and children with whom they could relate. Or, so many, possessing "profiles that resembled females in the general population" were drawn not by athletics but by aesthetics. As in the case of the fine arts and the fashion industry, where the predominance of gays is legendary, they gravitated to the "artsiness" of the liturgy and clerical lifestyles, which allows for flowing robes, lace surplices, lovely flowers, and elegant music.

Or finally, as some would argue, the whole system of the Catholic priesthood is inherently gay-styled. After all, the clergy are householders without wives, take on a number of domestic roles associated with women, dress in skirts, and act in public rituals that confuse gender roles as, arrayed in silk, they sing, act, and host a meal. Any other male doing what they're doing would be considered queer. Whatever the case, they were trained in a seminary, sometimes by homosexual priests, where the clerical culture of silence about anything human suppressed any discussions of sexuality, knew nothing of personality tests, and praised and awarded docility, conformity, and the "gentle" ways of the seminarian.

The exodus

In any case, contributing to the disproportionate number of gay priests is the exodus of heterosexual priests, those approximately 20,000 men in the United States who left to get married—and some left because they couldn't stand the flourishing gay subculture. This obviously has altered considerably the gay/straight ratio so that the homosexual proportion of the whole number went way up, while their absolute numbers stayed the same.

Whatever the arguments on either side, the stiff imbalance between the number of homosexual priests and heterosexual priests is at the heart of the anxiety about gay clergy. Whether motivated indeed by homophobic sentiments or merely desiring a more representative balance, many people are worried about the shift in numbers. And many worry about the polls that show that many gay priests do not observe celibacy but have lovers—often, like their gay counterparts in the secular community, many lovers. There are even, in Greeley's phrase, "networks" of gay priests. Some even had sex in the seminary. In a survey, 101 gay priests ordained after 1981 said their seminaries were seventy percent gay.

I think we can say that most laypeople are largely sympathetic and respectful to a priest who might be gay as long as he is a good and hardworking priest, keeps his vows, and does not become a part of any gay subculture. They would have a hard time, perhaps, if he hung out in gay singles bars. Still, the growing concern is that the priesthood of the future will likely be perceived as a gay profession. At some seminaries today, those who are about to be ordained have to go through rigorous counseling and have a proven record of continence. They must also exhibit habits that do not include gay contacts.

The point still remains that the disproportionate number of homosexually-oriented priests and seminarians, not to mention the presence of homosexuals on seminary faculties, statistically increases the actual and potential incidents of male sexual abuse. Furthermore that disproportionate number has to have some causal effect on the drastic reduction in the number of candidates for our seminaries. Also, if indeed almost half our priests and seminarians are homosexual then that also means that half our priests and seminarians are being recruited from roughly five to eight percent of the general population of American Catholic men.

The conclusion is obvious. Given the current context of a large number of gay priests, plus a critical need for clergy, it would seem to be wise to open up the priesthood to married men. It would seem the time, at this point in our history, to offer to all candidates the gift of celibacy along the lines Jesus himself suggested: "Not everyone can accept this teaching, but only those to whom it is given" (Mt 19:11).

It would also be the time to welcome back the many priests who have left to get married. After all, a Church that welcomes married Protestant ministers who converted to Catholicism and allows them to be ordained priests as married men should have no trouble welcoming its own. It would seem further that, in the current context of an all male clergy, when the clerical culture takes on a gay coloring it no longer represents the Church at large. And so the challenge here is to achieve a balance that does.

A parting comment comes back to the Church's biggest problem as we mentioned in the last chapter: the shortage of priests. If you subtract those priests who left to get married; then subtract those who would become priests except for the law of celibacy; then subtract those who would join the seminary but are put off by the current scandals; and then you further subtract all those priests against whom allegations have been made and who subsequently have been fired—some 176 so far (and the list grows longer every day)—then we have a full-blown disaster at hand. Celibacy, in this context alone, apart from theoretical considerations, begs to be optional if the Church is to survive. And so it is to celibacy we turn in the following chapter.

Questions for Discussion

1. By far, most of the abused are boys. The abusers are homosexual. Do you think this is a necessary or an accidental connection?

2. Did you ever realize that so many of the Catholic clergy were gay? How do you feel about this?

3. Do you think a gay man should be denied ordination? If so, why? If not, why?

EIGHT

Celibacy

His disciples said to him, "If such is the case of a man with his wife, it is better not to marry." But Jesus said to them, "Not everyone can accept this teaching, but only those to whom it is given. For there are eunuchs who have been so from birth, and there are eunuchs who have been made eunuchs by others and there are eunuchs who have made themselves eunuchs for the sake of he kingdom of heaven. Let anyone accept this who can." —Mt 19:10–12

There can be no doubt that the whole issue of abusing priests has raised more than ever the question of mandatory celibacy. In the height of the Boston scandal the diocesan newspaper, the *Pilot*, ran an editorial raising the question of whether the issue of celibacy should be revisited, whether there would be fewer scandals if celibacy were optional. A subsequent editorial denied that it wanted to challenge the policy of celibacy, which is a requirement for ordination (Canon 277). Still, the press picked up on this and those who have been campaigning for optional celibacy pounced on it.

As in the case of homosexuality, the right and the left are sharply divided on the issue of celibacy. Those on the right see a conspiracy to do away with celibacy. Those on the left call celibacy unnatural, impossible, and pathological. It is an issue that will be with us a long time. Meanwhile, from the viewpoint of linking celibacy and sexual abuse, there are some things to note.

First of all, child sexual abuse is not caused by celibacy. There is no evidence whatsoever to support that contention; even the proponents of optional celibacy admit that. The statistical fact is that the vast majority of sexual abuse cases of children and adolescents are by married men and women. The only thing we can say is that if sexual abuse is not caused by celibacy nevertheless, for some, celibacy can lead to sexual frustration and tension, which is why some celibates need help in learning how to deal with it.

Sexual abuse would be the result of celibacy only if it were not a problem among others working in the professions who have access to children. Most sexual abusers, as I said, are married. Also, as we saw, non-celibate clergy are just as likely to abuse; the statistics on Protestant and Jewish clergy who are abusers are not comforting. The simple fact is, then, that if the priest sexual abuser were married, he would still prey on children—perhaps, as often happens, his own children. Banning celibacy or making it optional is not of itself a cure for clerical sexual abuse. The tendency to abuse, as we saw, starts in the very early years and may express itself later whether one is married or not. The celibate priest doesn't become an abuser: the abuser becomes a celibate priest.

But concerning celibacy there are auxiliary concerns or "perumbas," as one Chief Justice so famously said, that make it an unsure charism for some. We can name three. For one thing, celibacy might appeal to and draw those unsure of their own sexuality. As Ronald Langevin, a psychologist at the University of Toronto says, some men may imagine that the priesthood will help them cope with their disorder and repress their sexual yearnings. Of course, it doesn't work that way. In other words, celibacy may offer an ideal environment for those men with an immature sexual identity. When the environment lets them down, so to speak, they may act out by preying on minors.

Second, there is the Catch-22 of celibacy, that is, a severe shortage of priests. This means that the large ordination classes are long gone. It also means that the old full-house rectory is long gone. As a result, the celibate priest has few or no classmates to socialize with. He often lives a solitary life in a house built for four or five. Where, then, does he turn for debriefing? With whom does he share his feelings, or even what his day was like? He becomes vulnerable to sympathetic ears, to the care and affections of laypeople, men or women, boys or girls.

Third, there is the whole question of context. I am talking now about the social-sexual revolution. Years ago, public sexual activity and pornography were unheard of. The environment was protective. You had to go out of your way to find dirty pictures. Movies were regulated. To say that is all changed is to grossly understate reality. Sex is practically a way of life. Abstinence is deemed sick and unhealthy.

Sex drives the movies, the Internet, magazines, fashion, and cosmetics. It sells everything from beer to mouthwash. It shapes our consciousness and unconsciousness. Spencer Tracy and Red Skelton have been replaced by Hugh Hefner and Jerry Springer, Molly Goldberg by Dr. Ruth. *The Honeymooners* have been replaced by *Sex in the City*. So some are asking, is it reasonable to keep celibacy as a requirement for ordination, given the nature of western culture? As Richard A. Gardner, professor of psychiatry at Columbia says,

> Perhaps such sexual inhibitions could be accomplished in a remote village in Ireland, Poland, and Italy where past exposure of sexual stimuli was limited. Today this is far less likely. From their earliest years, children are bombarded with sexual stimulation....The Church is misguided in believing it can take a young person who was brought up in this world, put him in a seminary, and fashion an asexual being.

Liberals who take this view have to be cautious, of course, lest they unintentionally offend the singles. Many single people, whether single by choice or circumstance, live good and productive lives. Are they to be categorized as sick, unreasonable, or pathological? Some are less sanguine and resent any talk about changing the law. The cynics chime in and say that if celibacy is "sick" as the more vocal put it, does anyone want to claim that its alternative, marriage, is "healthy"? The fact is that marriage has fallen out of favor. Statistically, for example, most Europeans do not get married but simply live together. The number of couples who live together in the United States has soared, as well. Half of those who do marry eventually divorce.

The matter of celibacy versus marriage for priests is not as simple as it sounds—although, for the record, seventy-seven percent of Catholics polled say they would be open to a married clergy. On the other hand, in a poll of Catholic priests taken in March, 2002, only twelve percent said they would get married if celibacy were optional, twelve percent were uncertain, and seventy-six percent said no, they would not get married if they could.

Whatever the argument on either side, the issue of celibacy may be entirely moot, for the case for optional celibacy rests on other, more pragmatic grounds. For one thing, given the extremely high percentage of gay clergy, optional celibacy that opened the door to heterosexuals would be welcomed to redress the imbalance. But the next reason is the telling one. And that reason, as I emphasized at the close of the last chapter, is that the Catholic priesthood is drying up. The numbers are beyond critical. They are disastrous. Given that severe shortage, which shows no signs of letting up, optional celibacy would seem a necessary choice.

Clergy shortage

Let's look into the clergy shortage. Notice, by the way, I emphasize the word "clergy" for all denominations are in shortfall. In the Episcopal Church, for example, which allows a married clergy, "the situation is grave," according to the Rev. Hugh Magers, a member of the congregational ministries cluster in Manhattan. In Reform Judaism there is a critical shortage of rabbis, and about 200 out of 895 congregations are without a full-time rabbi. Reform rabbinical ordination classes have dropped from having sixty candidates twenty years ago to only twenty today. Orthodox Judaism is experiencing the same shortage. The United Church of Christ, Disciples of Christ, the Lutherans, United Methodists, and all the rest are experiencing a shortage of clergy. Across the board, people are just not interested in becoming clergy, pointing out that entering the clerical life does not necessarily revolve around the issue of celibacy.

As I argued in my book, *Brave New Church*, with the numbers of Catholic clergy severely down, the sacramental life of the Church is in imminent danger of disappearing. The military, prison ministry, and parish life are all hurting for lack of priests. The thing is that the hierarchy has known about this shortage for many decades but has kept it under wraps. Social scientists were reporting the shortage as far back as 1970. In the 1980s the bishops, fully aware of declining numbers and with an endowment from the Lilly Foundation, commissioned a detailed research project, led by Richard Schoenherr, to study the situation. The resulting projections from the study were so alarming that in the early 1990s the bishops withdrew their sponsorship of the project. Nevertheless the report came out in 1993—and immediately the bishops stonewalled. They began to downplay the report, saying it was too pessimistic, too unhelpful, God would provide, and so on. Actually, the report was absolutely accurate in its findings that the priesthood was in serious decline.

Once again, we find that the bishops' reactive habit of secrecy is impossible for them to overcome. The shortage of priests, the number of homosexual seminarians and priests, the existence of clerical sexual abusers—they have known about all these issues for decades. Yet, they kept the information to themselves. Is it that they don't trust the laity to understand? Do they feel they have to protect "the sheep" at all costs? Can't they give the people credit for accepting and coming to terms with problems? Have they been so far removed from people that they don't know that people are understanding, that they will willingly and readily deal with a problem if they're told about it? Don't they trust the people? Apparently not. Now the people don't trust them.

Allow me to put a human face on this crisis by noting a few instances that may be close to your home: the Dubuque archdiocese, which had 286 priests in 1985, is projected to have only 117 in 2005. The Archdiocese of Boston announced that it ordained nine men in May of 1998. Such a number can't come near to replacing the twenty-five to thirty priests who have retired or died that same year.

Or, if you want to put it more dramatically, consider it this way: for the dioceses of Boston and New York combined, with four million Catholics and 800 parishes, only fourteen men were ordained in 1999. How about this: in the four years from 1997 to 2000, seven dioceses with a combined Catholic population of more than one million had no ordinations at all. In the Pittsburgh diocese, the number of active priests today is 371; only a decade ago it was 467, almost a hundred more. Directly citing the shortage of priests, the diocese of Evansville, Indiana, is planning to close or merge parishes, admitting that many people will have to travel fifteen to thirty minutes to find a Mass. The Archdiocese of Milwaukee, which ordained only one man in 1997 and one in 1998, lost thirty-four priests through retirement and resignation in the year 2000, and it will have lost 185 more by the year 2016. This diocese has already closed about forty parishes, with more closings to come.

The diocese of Toledo, Ohio, serves 325,000 Catholics in its 163 parishes with 200 active priests, far short of adequately meeting the needs of the people. The diocese expects to have fifty fewer priests in just six years. Thirty parishes are already served by visiting priests and six others have full-time, non-ordained leaders. The Archdiocese of Newark expects to have only 192 priests twenty years from now compared to the 540 it has today. Major archdioceses like Boston, New York, Chicago, and Los Angeles all ordained fewer than ten new priests in the year 2000.

Other grounds

To compound the priest shortage problem there are fewer and fewer seminarians to replace them. There has been an increase worldwide in seminarians—over some 40,000 since 1978—but they are mostly from Africa and Asia, and they are quickly absorbed in an ever-growing Catholic population. The western world is behind. In Canada, for example, there were 445 seminarians twenty years ago. Today there are forty-eight. There has been a minor upswing in vocations to the priesthood in the United States, but the fact still remains that for every one hundred men enrolled in Catholic seminaries in 1965 there are only forty today. From 1970 to 1995 seminary enrollment dropped by half. You don't have to be a mathematical genius to see that the priest shortage will obviously be with us a long time.

As a result of all this, priests are taking on two or more parishes, find themselves overworked (their chief complaint), and are aging. They live in oversized rectories alone or with one assistant, where previously they may have had three or four. Right now, over three thousand U.S. parishes are without a resident priest, and the number grows daily. People simply don't realize how bad the situation is and will be for a long time to come.

Since, in the Church's own declarations, "the salvation of souls...is always the supreme law of the Church" (Canon 1752) and "the liturgy is the summit towards which all activity of the Church is directed; it is also the font from which all her powers flow" (*Constitution on the Sacred Liturgy*), then to let these decline for the lack of male celibate priests is to seriously and reprehensibly undercut the whole mission of the Church. Besides, a married clergy is, as we all know, clearly in the tradition. Recall St. Paul's admonition to Timothy, that a bishop should be a man with a family and "a man of one woman"; in fact, beginning with Peter, the first pope, thirty-nine popes have been married.

Nor does the explosion of deacons and lay ministers settle the problem. They are of great help but still, the fact is that the sacramental life of anointing, absolving, and, most of all, celebrating the Eucharist belong to the priest. As his number declines, the sacramental life declines. Celibacy should not trump justice and charity; on these grounds alone the option for a married clergy is compelling.

In fact, so serious is the priest shortage that it raises an intriguing scenario. Consider this: canon law (Canons 883:3, 884:2, and 976) says that where there is danger of death or other emergencies, keeping the pastoral needs of the people always in mind, priests currently without faculties can hear confession, administer confirmation, and anoint the sick. The question then becomes this: when the people are without a priest and are in danger of dying without the sacraments; when they will be denied the Eucharist for a long time, does the parish have a moral obligation to print in its bulletin a list of already married priests? Can the people, long without Mass—an obvious pastoral emergency—turn to them? Will a married clergy come in this way, through the back door, so to speak?

It would be foolish, of course, to deny the practical problems of transitioning to a married clergy. There would be such problems as finances (at a time when many dioceses are near bankruptcy), housing, divorce (a bane of the Protestant clergy; what you do with a divorced priest?), the loss of easy transfers, rectory access, camaraderie, and so on. And anyone who thinks that a married clergy would dissolve the so-called "clerical culture" should visit our Protestant brethren's conferences.

There would be the danger, too, of a certain loss of appreciation for the charism of celibacy itself. A society that glorifies all kinds of sexual expression, where even, as we said, the country's major corporations are heavily invested in the pornography industry, celibacy is considered to have no place—this, in spite of the fact that the majority of celibates keep their vows and live productive lives. One thinks of Mother Teresa, Pope John XXIII, and Father Mychal Judge, who was among the first to die in administering the last rites to victims of the World Trade Center disaster.

When you come right down to it, celibacy is about love. It's an ancient tradition, prized by many societies. It's all about loving deeply, about being a sign of unity in a fragmented world. It's not a better or worse way of loving than being married, but it has its place and that place should not be lost or denigrated. In our own society, one that produces widespread divorce, devastating diseases like AIDS, betrayed spouses, teenage pregnancies, fatherlessness, and celebrated promiscuity, celibacy stands out as a powerful sign and witness to love.

We do not want to lose an appreciation for celibacy. Nevertheless, for those to whom such a gift has not been given or freely chosen, the option to marry should be allowed, particularly when the people of God are starving for the Eucharist and that hunger could be fed by a married clergy. The thing is, we have had a married clergy for many years in our history. And so the question remains: is it time for history to repeat itself?

Questions for Discussion

1. Some say that, in the light of the scandals, celibacy should be made optional. What do you think?

2. Do you favor a married clergy?

3. Would you be willing to support a married priest and his family?

4. Do you have any experience of Protestant married clergy?

How has marriage and their profession worked for them?

5. Some men want to become priests but also want to be married, and so they do not become priests. Others want to become priests but shy away because of the scandals. Still others who are already priests have been dismissed because of allegations of misconduct. That leaves an already depleted clergy even smaller. Did you realize the shortage of priests is so critical?

6. There are some 20,000 priests in the United States who have left to get married. Would you be in favor of taking them back into active ministry?

NINE

Holy Week 2002

Now, before the festival of the Passover, Jesus knew that his hour had come to depart from this world and go to the Father. Having loved his own who were in the world he loved them to the end. —Jn 13:1

The days of Holy Week 2002 took on a special poignancy for priests. Burdened with shame for their brethren and laden with suspicion themselves, they inexorably felt themselves drawn into the drama of that week as never before in their lives. As in a surreal dream, they found themselves there that week in the very heart of betrayal, pain, and turmoil. Each day of Holy Week wore the face of The Scandal. Allow me to share, in this brief chapter, our thoughts.

Wednesday of Holy Week

And from that moment he began to look for an opportunity to betray him. —Mt 26:16

In the misty fog of their subconscious minds, priests envisioned their Judas this day. Yes, there he was, one of their number, part of their band, one they had broken bread with, joked with, met at Forty Hours and penance services, saw at meetings. Nothing to mark him out as a traitor; the eleven were not aware of Judas as anything other than one of them.

They see him now with fresh eyes. Shockingly, there he is, like Judas, looking for the time, means, and opportunity to betray Jesus in the person of an innocent boy. There he is, the family's parish priest, friend, and confidant. There are his treats, his dropping over to the house, his little presents, his hanging around with the kids, his smile, his role as trusted friend. He is one of the privileged and respected twelve. Then, somewhere along the line, Satan enters into his heart. There first comes the sweet talk—it is almost too painful to watch—then the first fumbling touches, then the violation.

When it is all over, there is the persuasion that "this is our little secret." "Just between ourselves, okay?" "God gives only very special people the opportunity to do these things with a priest." "You can't tell. Nobody would ever believe you anyway." Innocence is shattered. The betrayal is complete. And it will happen over and over again. It is hard to endure Judas this Wednesday.

Holy Thursday

Then he poured water into basin and began to wash the disciples' feet and to wipe them with the towel that was tied around him. —Jn 13:5

In the dream world of priests on Holy Thursday, when they came to the traditional washing of the feet and looked up, shockingly, there were not twelve adults. Good God, there were twelve children: children with looks of disbelief, shame, confusion, and bewilderment on their faces. Their arms were folded across their chests as if to protect themselves. Their eyes were searching. Their ears were turned as if waiting to hear some explanation, some reason why this happened to them.

At this point, the priests, like Jesus, took upon themselves the sins of the world. So on that Holy Thursday of 2002, they assumed the role of the abuser. They bent over the children's feet, took them gently and let their tears replace the water. They sobbed over and over again, "I am sorry. I am sorry. Forgive me. Forgive me. Forgive me for breaking trust, forgive me for stealing your innocence. Forgive me for giving you bad dreams and sleepless nights. Forgive me for twisting your life, for repressing your memories, for causing you pain. I, your abuser, am sorry." And they wept all the more, long and hard.

Then, just as quickly as they took on the role of abuser, the priests, still bending over those childish feet, suddenly found their heads weighted with a miter. A ring is on their fingers. They are bishops. They are the institutional Church. And they find themselves mouthing a new refrain. "I am sorry for my insensitivity, for covering up, for not taking the blame, for evading the truth. I am sorry for sending you one I knew had hurt other children. I am sorry for intimidating you, for offering you everything from compensation to false promises except the one thing you wanted to hear: that I am consummately, profoundly sorry for what has happened to you. I apologize. I am ready to take whatever comes my way, even imprisonment. I have been wrong, terribly, terribly wrong. Can you ever forgive me?"

And, in that fantasy, the priests took off their rings and miters and put on sackcloth and ashes and prostrated themselves before the children and before the world. And in that fantasy also, the priests-now-bishops found themselves announcing to the world the formation of a new religious order: the Order of Penitent Bishops who, having resigned, gather in community and devote themselves to prayer and fasting and works of mercy.

Good Friday

Those who passed by derided him. —Mt 27:39

Good Friday was a troublesome day for Catholics, especially for priests. There were many things to resonate with this day. Priests were angry that the Church allowed the abuse to continue so long. They felt, as did many of the laity, that the Church is as guilty in handing over innocent children to a known pedophile as those who falsely accused Jesus, as those who shouted for his condemnation, as those who cried "Crucify him! Crucify him!"

Priests were pained as they felt the stares of even their own parishioners. They hesitated to go out wearing a Roman collar. They suddenly felt what Peter was feeling around that fire that day. "You too are one of them!" And they were tempted to curse and swear, "I know not the man! I'm not part of that company that abuses children!" And they went out and wept bitterly for the sins of their brothers. They experienced that year that their brotherhood, like Christ on the cross, was exposed in all its fragility and ugliness. Spit, flogging, thorns, blood, the stench of death are there. And, as always, the jeers of those passing by: national vulgarian Howard Stern, after porn star Rebecca Lord stripped naked while condemning the Church on his TV show, shouted, "Catholic priests are having sex with young boys!" Columnist Maureen Dowd: "We now have a perp walk of sacramental perverts." More voices, many more, joined in the mockery. It was hard to bear. Never more have the priests felt the force of Isaiah's words:

> He had no form or majesty that we should look at him,
> Nothing in his appearance that we should desire him. He was
> despised and rejected by others; a man of suffering and
> acquainted with infirmity; and as one from whom others hide
> their faces he was despised, and we held him of no account.
> (53:2–3)

Holy Saturday

> *Joseph took the body… and laid it in his own new tomb.*
> —Mt 27:59–60

There is no life. All is lifeless this day. The priests feel numb, numb as that dead body in the tomb, for each day brings a new revelation of abuse, another name exposed, another resignation, another sidelong glance. Will it ever stop? Will we ever heal? The Church seems dead, dead as the body of Christ resting in the arms of his anguished mother. A refrain from the *Stabat Mater* readily comes to mind:

> Is there one who would not weep,
> Whelmed by miseries so deep,
> Christ's dear mother to behold?

> Can the human heart refrain
> From partaking in her pain
> In that mother's pain untold?

Is there one who would not weep? There are more than enough tears to go around. Tears for the victims and their families, who must live with the scars forever. Tears for the bishops who stonewalled. Tears for the priests who did the terrible deeds. Tears for the accused priest in Ireland who drove his car over a cliff. Tears for the accused priest in Ohio who sat in his car and blew his brains out. Tears for their mothers and fathers now doubly disgraced. Tears for their stunned parishes who must bury them.

It seems as if a large stone has sealed the priesthood, the Church, forever. The question that lodged in the hearts of the priest and his parishioners that year was "Who will roll away the stone?" (Mk 16:3).

Holy Week in the year 2002 was difficult.

Questions for Discussion

1. Can you feel what it must be like to be a priest these days?

2. Guilt by association is the burden of the priest today. Can you sense it?

3. Have you affirmed your parish priest lately?

TEN

Galvanized

I give thanks to my God always for you because of the grace of God that has been given to you in Christ Jesus, for in every way you have been enriched in him, in speech and knowledge of every kind. —1 Cor. 1:4

One thing that is clear from all this terrible scandal is that the clerical culture is in demise. As much as anything, the crisis we're going through is a crisis of leadership, one that revolves around the hierarchical structure in the Church today. It is a crisis of trust and credibility, of confidence in our bishops and priests.

That is why, from this point on, there will be a whole new emphasis on accountability. No more will deep secrets that impact the people be buried. There will be much more lay collaboration and input and, to a certain degree, overseeing. A current example comes from the Diocese of Rockville Centre, New York, which announced that non-Catholics and law enforcement experts would help in future allegations of sexual abuse by priests. I'll repeat what I said above: the clerical culture, as we have known it, that last remnant of a medieval lifestyle, is being dismantled. That culture of privilege, exemption, status, and secrecy is toppling. The strict hierarchy with priest over laity, bishop over priest, and pope over bishop is melting. This, perhaps, will be the ultimate casualty of the scandal—and it's long overdue.

As an acquaintance of mine put it, the laity are not traumatized; they are galvanized. The laity recognize it is not faith that is at stake here, but Church management. Even up in war-torn Boston, ninety-one percent of those interviewed said their faith was not diminished by the events there. The laity have pinpointed the real problem: the Church's image was more important than its children.

Another year!—another deadly blow!
Another mighty Empire overthrown!
And we are left, or shall be left, alone.

Not for the laity to buy into Wordsworth's refrain. They are rising up with slogans of taking back the Church. Liberal and conservative Catholics all agree on one thing: there is no going back for the Church. They see the present crisis as an opportunity for change, if not a mandate. Therefore, their voices have never been louder. They are jettisoning a culture "of extreme clerical deference." They are openly criticizing their leaders from the pope on down.

Polls show that U.S. Catholics and indeed Americans in general give the hierarchy poor marks for the way they have handled the scandal. As for Rome, she has let them down too many times, especially on the birth control issue; what the pope said on this matter, ignoring his advisors, was promptly and universally rejected. "Rome," or curial pronouncements, though listened to with respect, just doesn't command total allegiance anymore. There is an old Latin saying, *Roma locuta est. Causa finita est*; "Rome has spoken. The case is closed." The average American Catholic today responds, "Forget it. The discussion is just beginning."

Most winningly of all, however, the people are making distinctions between their pastors' lives and service and that of the hierarchy. They have a keen sense of appreciation for the priests who are struggling to keep their communities together (a sixty-five percent approval rating as against only forty percent for the hierarchy). They express overwhelming confidence in their parish priests, indicating that they feel the priests are really in touch with the needs of the modern Catholics. And even those who are withholding their contributions are withholding them only from the chancery or the Vatican (the next Peter's Pence will be a bust); but they are increasing donations to their local parishes.

In turn the parish priests themselves are galvanizing. They too are openly challenging their bishops. They are meeting in groups by themselves and speaking out loud what was formerly forbidden. They are openly talking about celibacy, a married clergy, and homosexual priests, and they are finding a way to frame the conversation about gay priests as caring, competent servants. They have and are continuing to have open sessions with their people. In a word, the parish priests too are engaged in a major mental shift. No longer are they slavishly deferential to their bishops. They have switched their primary allegiance to their people.

What all this portends is that, from now on, there will be a new openness, with the people participating in forming policies. Pastoral councils and priests' senates will be strengthened. And the prohibition against even talking openly about problems and issues will no longer hold. It never did anyway since the invention of the printing press and surely it does not now with the arrival of the Internet, where everything is up for grabs.

In fact, during this whole crisis people have been deluging popular religious websites like beliefnet.com. The gist of their chat room exchanges has been how relieved they are to be able to talk about this scandal in the open, to express their opinions and learn more about what's happening. The bishops are naïve if they think that anything from now on is off limits for discussion. That is why their silence on critical issues has proven disastrous. They didn't even discuss issues with their own priests, the men in the front line who were bidden in effect to defend the indefensible. What we're taking about is a whole new restructuring of the Church.

Moreover, various voices, such as those of minorities and women, are now being heard and listened to, and there is on every level much more collaboration than there has been. Many parishes already function in this way and they are alive and flourishing. Shared and collaborative ministry—clergy and laity alike in a joint effort to bring the kingdom of God to all—will be the norm. The clerical culture is over. The discipleship of all is in. The voices of the people will be heard as never before. If anything good will come out of this tragedy, it is that.

The front line

I detected this resiliency and determination of the people in a headline in the New York *Times* on Easter Sunday: "Parish Embraces a Time of Hope, Not Scandal." The article went on to tell about the parishioners in a parish in Wisconsin who, aware of and fretting over the scandals of so many abusive priests, were in church to draw a renewed faith from the themes of Holy Week. A sense of deceit, abandonment, betrayal, and death was there as well, all too familiar. But there was also the resurrection; this was Easter and indeed, the people were there to embrace hope. In fact, all around the country, the churches on Easter 2002 seemed more full than ever.

The remarkable fact is that, although sad and angry, the Catholic people are still keeping faith. Many simply love the Church and would never dream of leaving it. In the *Times* article, a few of the people interviewed said their faith was shaken. Some remarked that a priest or a bishop or a cardinal is only human. Others were glad it was being talked about as many priests raised the subject at Holy Week and Easter Masses. Most often, people talked about the Church in terms of family and said things like this: it's a dysfunctional family and we've got to fix it; or, it's like having arguments among troubled relatives but no one's ready to disown the family; or, after all, it's Holy Mother Church, and even when your mother errs or you get angry with her, she's still your mother and you're bound to her with lasting ties.

I wonder if the bishops are listening. Do they realize that the Church is made up of such a stalwart, faithful people, who make better distinctions than they realize? I am reminded of a great man of decades ago, Frank Sheed, father, author, theologian, who was privy to many secrets in the Church. With an eye to history, he wrote:

> We are not baptized into the hierarchy; do not receive the cardinals sacramentally; will not spend an eternity in the beatific vision of the pope. St. John Fisher could say in a public sermon, "If the pope will not reform the curia, God will." A couple of years later he laid his head on Henry VIII's block for papal supremacy, followed to the same block by Thomas More, who had spent his youth under the Borgia pope, Alexander VI, lived his early manhood under the Medici pope, Leo X, and died for papal supremacy under Clement VII, as time-serving a pope as Rome ever had. Christ is the point.

> I myself, admire the present pope but even if I criticized

him as harshly as some do, even if his successor proved to be as bad as some of those who have gone before, even if I sometimes find the Church as I have to live with it, a pain in the neck, I should still say that nothing a pope [or a priest] could do or say would make me wish to leave the Church, although I might well wish that he would leave.

Israel, through its best periods as through its worst, preserved the truth of God's oneness in a world swarming with gods, and a sense of God's majesty in a world sick with its own pride. So with the Church. Under the worst administration we could still learn Christ's truth, receive his life in the sacraments, be in union with him to the limit of our willingness. In awareness of Christ, I can know the Church as his mystical body, and we must not make our judgment by the neck's sensitivity to pain.

I think people have an instinctive appreciation of this truth. No one—no pope, no bishop, no priest—can completely erase the face of Christ or undo his mission. Grace is still amazing even among the revelations of scandal. Renewal is larger than sin, faith is stronger than scandal, and hope is greater than despair. Jesus is simply too strong, too "risen" to be undone by a new set of Judases. It been tried, alas, too many times in history, and Jesus has prevailed.

The people will be the ones to roll back the stone. True enough, there is the realization that the Church will never be the same again after this most serious crisis since it came to the New World. But people have sensed that seeds have been planted in the dirt of scandal, seeds that will renew the Church. Let me mention some of these seeds and the hope they give.

New policies

First of all, the bishops, chastened, are more and more doing sincerely what they should have done from the beginning. They are speaking openly about the scandals. They are publicly apologizing. True, they may have been embarrassed into it, but take it as a step forward. They are making heartfelt apologies to the victims and to the people at large. And they are doing this freely and feelingly. They are appearing before the people as penitent. And that is a new stance not to be despised.

Second, open and well-publicized policies are being put into practice. Soon the bishops will have a national policy for all dioceses, but most of them have local ones. They all pretty much cover the same ground and include the following principles:

1. All allegations of sexual abuse are immediately reported to the civil authorities. This has become the law in many states.

2. Allegations are first addressed with the welfare of the victim in mind, not the interests of the Church.

3. The accused is immediately removed from assignment pending the outcome of an investigation.

4. Victims and their families are offered pastoral care and professional counseling.

5. Prevention procedures will be put into practice, such as carefully screening new seminarians and background checks on newly hired employees, teachers, and new volunteers who work with children

Some dioceses will soon have a hotline to call and a website to tap.

Third, seminarian formation is being vastly improved—at least in some seminaries. It is no longer either permitted or desired, as it was in the recent past, to take in "anyone over eighteen who is breathing" in order to fill depleting ranks.

Actually, it didn't take the current scandal to call attention to the necessity of raising the quality of seminarians or to revise the seminary curriculum and the standards for admission. Once again, back as far as 1972, the National Conference of Catholic Bishops authorized a series of detailed and extensive investigations into the priesthood. The study concluded that fully one-third of the priests were underdeveloped emotionally, one-third were developing, and one-third were developed. Around the same time, psychologist Eugene Kennedy found that fifty-seven percent were underdeveloped. It would come as no surprise that some of them could not handle their sexual feelings. A familiar cry: too bad some bishops didn't heed the report they themselves had commissioned. The result was that some bishops accepted less than stable men, sometimes against the recommendation of the seminary staff. We have been paying for their choices.

Those entering the seminaries today, however, are subject to strict scrutiny and psychological evaluation. In some seminaries (not all yet, unfortunately) their backgrounds are checked carefully. They have been subject to Rorschach tests and criminal background checks, and they have been interviewed about their dating history and sexual orientation. They are offered courses on sexuality and addiction. Their intellectual and spiritual training is challenging and ongoing. Their commitment to celibacy is strong.

Many of them are quite mature, having chosen the clerical life as a second career. And they are not the children of the freewheeling sixties as most of the priest sexual abusers were. They have seen firsthand some of the excesses. They have seen their friends, siblings, and sometimes their own parents divorce in record numbers. Having been raised in a neutral, nonjudgmental, hands-off religious milieu, they are hungry for God—as are many of their contemporaries. They are seekers and leaders. Their training is different today. *They* are different. And even though some who are recently ordained seem lacking in some areas, the future looks more hopeful.

Finally, the nation's Catholic schools have inaugurated sex abuse prevention lessons for children from as early as age five. Actually such programs began appearing in the 1980s after the scandals of that time, programs like Good Touch, Bad Touch, and Safe Touch. These programs are being intensified and upgraded. Here's the bottom line: we're moving on.

Questions for Discussion

1. To say that things will be different from now on is an understatement. What would you do to reform the Church?

2. Has your parish priest talked about the scandal from the pulpit? Has your parish had open meetings on the subject?

3. Are you aware of the policies in your diocese for reporting sexual abuse by the clergy?

4. Do you know any seminarians? Do they strike you as being men of good quality?

ELEVEN

Bishops and Trust

[A bishop] must be well thought of by outsiders, so that he may not fall into disgrace and the snare of the devil. —1 Tim 3:7

Although there are many fine and good bishops individually, collectively they have been woefully inadequate to say the least. The previous pages have testified amply to this. They have exhibited a collective mentality of subservience to Rome and an unawareness of their people's basic needs. They became captive to all that is enshrined in the phrase, "good ol' boys club." Perhaps too inbred, they lost touch and talked only to one another. Some were subverted by their ambition. Others were compromised by politics. Others drowned in the ocean of bureaucracy. How else can you explain their failures even by their own moral terms? Look again at the record.

The bishops knew the existence not only of many homosexuals in the priesthood and in the seminaries, but also of the fact that many of them were unchaste. They looked the other way. They knew of sexually abusive priests yet they did not inform the Catholic public even when they moved predators from place to place. They held fast to the ideal of celibacy but were quite aware that many priests were not observing it. They too chuckled knowingly over the old joke about the cardinal who said that celibacy would never be dropped in his lifetime but it would be in his children's.

They did not dialogue collectively with those 20,000 priests in this country who left to get married. They were painfully aware for many decades of the growing shortage of priests but buried their heads in the sand. They did nothing to prepare or alert the people.

Right up to late 1990s they were using the public relations phrase, "the pastoral concern over the declining number of priests." It was only at their June meeting in the year 2000 that they went public and said the "s" word: shortage. They saw their parishes go priest-less, their aging priests become overworked. Their response was to come up with strategies to combine parishes, mandate large church buildings, and take away the Eucharist from the people. And although everyone in the world was talking about these issues, they bowed to Rome's pressure not to discuss in any sympathetic way contraception, celibacy, or the ordination of women.

What I am saying is that we have a crisis of leadership. And it's not just the present scandal that brought it on. Today's crisis of leadership is the result of the long, slow, steady pattern over the past fifty years of being out of touch with the people and with the things that concern them. It's the cumulative effect of the bishops' indifference, incompetence, and unwillingness to share, to openly discuss vital issues with the people. It's the long-term result of the bishops' habit of resorting to ecclesiastical jargon and retreating into the clerical boardroom. It's the long-held impression by the people that the bishops were totally mystified over their everyday concerns, almost, at times, contemptuous of their needs.

If only the bishops had followed their better instincts; if only they had taken seriously the very studies they themselves had mandated instead of killing the messengers; if only they had listened to the voice of the people. Here is a sample of what they might have heard:

A former Kansas City-St. Joseph vicar general, Father Norman Rotert, a priest for forty-two years, spoke with considerable candor at a 1995 luncheon talk to the Catholic Press Association: "The shortage of priests is not going to be solved by gritting our teeth and praying for more vocations. Women are the ones who identify and nurture vocations, and they are not doing it anymore and they are not going to do it. If you don't believe me, talk to them. I've interviewed them. They say, A Church that won't accept my daughters isn't going to get my son.' 'I know my son has a vocation to the priesthood but he won't accept celibacy.' 'I don't want my sons to go through what you and other priests have had to go though since the pedophilia issue surfaced.'"

Rotert's candid remarks reminded me of a conversation with a priest colleague who, like most of us on the seminary faculty, did supply work on weekends. After Mass one Sunday morning, a young man approached him and said he might be interested in the priesthood. Apparently prepared for just such a moment, the priest handed him some vocation materials. Suddenly his mother stood between them and grabbed the pamphlet from her son's hand. Throwing it down, she said with a voice of steel, "No son of mine is going to be a damn priest!" Perhaps surprised at her own vehemence, she added, "Nothing against you, Father. It's just that no son of mine is going to be a priest."

This kind of anger isn't often evident to priests greeting people after Eucharist on Sunday mornings, but it is there nonetheless. It matters little whether priests feel it is unfair and unwarranted, whether it's displaced or disproportionate. This mother's angry response falls into context, however, when viewed in the light of a recent CARA report sponsored by the National Conference of Catholic Bishops. When asked to react to the statement "You would encourage your child to pursue a career as priest or nun," parents' response fell into the following four categories: agree, twenty-five percent; strongly agree, eight percent; disagree, forty-eight percent; and strongly disagree, nineteen percent. A staggering sixty-seven percent disagreed or strongly disagreed with the statement. Only thirty-three percent agreed or strongly agreed. The angry mother in question apparently has a good deal of company.

In light of this report, one in five Catholic parents would strongly resist a child pursuing a vocation to the priesthood or religious life. Evidence that two-thirds would withhold encouragement to a son or daughter considering a vocation underscores the challenge facing vocation directors and seminary recruiters. It also reveals an important factor in the vocation crisis that is regularly overlooked. Catholics, in stark contrast to parents of previous generations, are no longer likely to see priesthood and religious life as a healthy way of life for their children. (Donald Cozzens, *The Changing Face of the Priesthood*)

Mind and heart

Did the bishops ever hear this voice of the people? Perhaps, as someone somewhat radically suggested, a third of them should resign every three years and let in new blood. We need not go that far, but there is no doubt that, under pressure from the current disgrace, under the close scrutiny of the laity, the criteria for choosing our leaders will change, *must* change.

Orthodoxy, connections, and efficiency will no longer be the sole standards for choosing bishops. (I don't think we can eradicate politics altogether). We will seek men who are bright but who also have heart. The powerful words of Chaim Potok in his book, *The Chosen*, stand as a searing indictment of what has been:

> Reuven, the Master of the Universe blessed me with a brilliant son. And he cursed me with all the problems of raising him. Ah, what it is to have a brilliant son! Not a smart son, Reuven, but a brilliant son, Daniel, a boy with a mind like a jewel. Ah, what a curse it is, what an anguish it is to have a Daniel whose mind is like a pearl, like a sun. Reuven, when my Daniel was four years old, I saw him reading a story. He swallowed it as one swallows food or water. There was no soul in my four-year-old Daniel, there was only his mind. He was a mind in a body without a soul. It was a story in a Yiddish book about a poor Jew and his struggle to get to Eretz Yisroel before he died. Ah, how that man suffered! And my Daniel enjoyed the story. He enjoyed the last terrible page, because when he finished it, he realized for the first time what a memory he had. He looked at me proudly and told me the story from memory, and I cried inside my heart.
>
> I went away and cried to the Master of the Universe. "What have you done to me? A mind like this I need for a son? A heart I need for a son, a soul I need for a son. Compassion I want from my son, righteousness, mercy, strength to suffer and carry pain, that I want from my son, not a mind without a soul!"

Compassion, righteousness, mercy, strength to suffer and carry the people's pain—that's what we want as criteria for our bishops, not minds without souls.

But therein lies the problem. Our crisis is not only with our bishops but also with the quality of the men we have. And this has been created by a system of episcopal appointments by Rome, which favors career-minded, docile men. And even where the bishops were forthright the Vatican shut them down, denied their requests, and in effect made them powerless. It took any clout away from the bishops' conferences and made them rubber stamps.

Now, in the context of our current scandal and this crisis of leadership, we want a voice in how our bishops are chosen: I think that will come. I have written elsewhere several times criticizing the system of picking bishops. The current system works like this: the local bishop secretly sends three names of potential candidates to Rome. (There's that secrecy again. The people whose leader he will be have no inkling of who is being considered.) The bishop, of course, is going to pick men he can trust—in other words, men who are like him and share his values. Prophets need not apply. The pope then makes his choice.

Most of the bishops in the world today have been chosen by Pope John Paul II. They are not bold. They have not spoken out favorably on any forbidden issues. They are conservatively orthodox. They are often chosen from administration, devoid of any real pastoral experience. In past books I have urged as a requirement that episcopal candidates must have been in parish work for at least ten years and not just as weekend help. They must have experienced the people firsthand. Moreover, the people at every parish a candidate has worked at should be polled as to his pastoral style and sensitivity. I would go even further. Like the threefold publication of banns for engaged couples, every diocesan paper throughout the land should be required to publish the banns of candidates for the office of bishop. This way we might avoid another situation like the one that occurred in the diocese of Palm Beach, Florida, noted in a previous chapter.

In the fifth century Pope Celestine I said, "No bishop is to be imposed on unwilling subjects, but the consent and wishes of clergy and people are to be considered." In that same century, Pope Leo added, "On no account is anyone to be bishop who has not been chosen by the clergy, desired by the people, and consecrated by the bishops of the province." A sixth-century Church council declared, "No one is to be consecrated as a bishop unless the clergy and the people of the diocese have been called together and have given their consent."

Maybe it's time to return to the ancient wisdom. A galvanized laity would like that.

Questions for Discussion

1. The bishops and the Vatican have been wrong. They are a part of a closed clerical culture that is breaking down. What would you put in its place?

2. What qualities would you like to see in a bishop?

3. What do you think of the suggestion that potential bishops must first be seasoned pastors and that the people of the parish be polled as to his stewardship?

4. What do you think of the suggestion of posting banns for potential episcopal candidates?

TWELVE

Soul Survivors

You are a chosen race, a royal priesthood, a holy nation, God's own people. —1 Peter 2:9

As I write this final chapter—an epilogue, really—the scandal still goes on. After all these weeks, the nightly news still carries stories about abusive priests. Networks run hour-long specials on the scandal. Lawyers and victims, motivated by sincere justice or common greed, continue to come forward with new allegations. More perpetrators are revealed. Prosecutors now have almost carte blanche access to the file of every priest who has been accused in the past half-century. There is an inevitable slide to this witch hunt. As someone said, it's like being on page fifty of a five-hundred-page Russian novel: there's a lot more to come.

And all of this comes on top of ongoing, overall declines in the Church. The number of nuns has vanished almost to extinction, and the ones who are left are elderly. As we have seen, the priesthood is quickly disappearing. Young Catholics still like being Catholic but, by all measurements, are far removed from the institutional Church and even further from its teachings.

Church attendance has declined almost seventy percent in the last few decades. The Church is paying out almost a billion dollars in compensation to victims, thus hindering the charitable works of its institutions and schools. The Church is still reeling from the recent and vigorous accusations of deep systemic anti-Semitism. No doubt about it, in the third millennium of Christianity, the Church sits like Job on the dunghill awaiting the next bit of bad news. What's left?

What's left, as we have seen throughout this book, is the people. What's left is you, the reader. You are what I call "soul survivors." I have taken that phrase from a fine evangelical Christian writer, Philip Yancey, who has written a book of that same name. The phrase, besides being a play on words, is accurate. Yancey, a Southerner, was dismayed to find deep racism, narrowness, lying, cover-ups, pettiness, and division in his churches. His first chapter is aptly titled, "Recovering from Church Abuse." His opening lines, which could easily be put into the mouths of Catholics, are a gem:

> Sometimes in a waiting room or on an airplane I strike up a conversation with strangers, during the course of which they learn that I write books on spiritual themes. Eyebrows arch, barriers spring up, and often I hear yet another horror story about church. My seatmates must expect me to defend the church because they always act surprised when I respond, "Oh, it's even worse than that. Let me tell you my story." I have spent most of my life in recovery from the church.

How can you not love a man like that? How did he survive? He survived by turning to representatives of the faith, flawed people who rose to heroism, and whose words and actions he found to be Christianity at its best. So he profiles eleven people who showed him how to live a Christlike life in spite of scandalous leaders. The ones he chooses to write about range from flawed Martin Luther King, Jr., to the robust G.K. Chesterton, the Indian Mahatma Gandhi to the Japanese Shusaku Endo, from the drunken Fyodor Dostoevsky to the chaste homosexual priest Henri Nouwen. In the witness of these lives and those like them, he found true Christianity.

I venture to say that the situation today is something like what happened in the early Church. There the question was always this: how did a tiny group of radical people on the fringe of the Roman empire, without hierarchy as we know it, without canon law and complex structures, palatial dwellings, the Vatican, curia, and large cathedrals—how did they become the dominant religion of western civilization? The answer is, through the witness of the average person. Their prayer life, their devotion to the Eucharist, their willingness to be countercultural to the point of martyrdom and, above all, their patient charity, which forced even their enemies to grudgingly admit, "See those Christians, how they love one another," was the answer.

This historic example tells us that we can't merely stand around pointing fingers at erring priests and bishops. If we, like Yancey, are to be in recovery from the Church, change must begin with us. The witness of us soul survivors will turn the tide. Whatever is happening "upstairs," however long this current scandal continues to shock our minds and sear our souls, the survival of the Church is up to us. We are the Church. It will become too facile to keep on blaming our leaders. We have to admit that we have been too passive as Catholics. Perhaps that's due to our training, our conditioning, our upbringing. We did not critique our priests or push for their removal if they were inadequate or criminal. We did not withhold our contributions in order to send a message. But that's all changed now. There is an emerging consensus among us that we have power, that we will stand against poor priests and in great solidarity with the good ones.

Every crisis is basically a crisis of holiness. That is why we must not only be disgusted but we must be holy. We must not only be angry but we must be moral. We must not only be hurt but we must be openly charitable. We must not opt out of the Church but give it a new face. On the street where we live people must be forced to pause and say to themselves, "See those Catholics, how they love one another." Our confidence, grounded in the moral life, that all will be well, must be predicated on a Christlike life. Then, and only then, our holy defiance, our mandate for change, will gain legitimacy and enable us to boldly and confidently shout to the world:

> Who shall separate us from the love of Christ? Will hardship or distress or persecution, or famine, or nakedness, or peril, or sword....No, in all these things we are more than conquerors through him who loved us. For I am convinced that neither death, nor life, nor angels, nor rulers, nor things present, nor things to come, nor powers nor height, nor depth, nor anything else in all creation will be able to separate us from the love of God in Christ Jesus our Lord. (Rom 8:35–39)

That's a galvanized laity!

Questions for Discussion

1. People in the Catholic Church today are loyal, and they are galvanized. Do you feel that way?

2. Rebuilding will come from the ground up; that is, from the witness of people like you. Do you agree?

APPENDIX I

Questions
& Answers

This section expands and updates the material in the text and reflects frequently asked questions.

Q. *Corporations also stonewall, do they not?*
A. Yes, they surely do. If priests have seldom been jailed for the criminal offense of sexual abuse (soon to change, as we indicated in chapter three), we should remember that such protection is rampant in corporate life. I recommend that you take a look, for example, at the March 18, 2002 issue of *Fortune* magazine, where Clifton Lea catalogues the endless instances of corporate thievery. He states that many executives, who have cheated the public out of millions and millions of dollars, go scott free:

> Before Enronitis inflamed the public, gigantic, white-collar swindlers were rolling through the business world and the legal system with their customary regularity. And though they displayed the full creative range of executive thievery, they had one thing in common. Hardly anyone ever went to prison.

Q. *Why do dioceses use hardball tactics such as those you mentioned in chapter two?*
A. We did mention the legal stonewalling reactions of the Church. In fairness, however, it should be noted that very few dioceses

have legal departments. Therefore, the ones who handle Church suits are the lawyers from the insurance companies. They, of course, use every hardball corporate trick to limit liability and protect the assets of the Church. This is why dioceses have acted no differently from commercial institutions that are sued. Now, whether the Church should have allowed the insurance lawyers to take over and play rough is another matter.

Q. *You've referred to the clergy shortage. What caused it? We had so many priests in the 1940s and '50s. What happened?*
A. Remember: the shortage is across the board, as all denominations are feeling it. A thumbnail response would include: the new attitudes which began in the 1960s; distrust of authority figures (and the priest is one); the tyrannies of the sexual revolution, where sex came to be regarded as a right, chastity a defect, and celibacy a pathology; the withdrawal of so many heterosexual priests to get married, and the resulting pool of homosexual seminarians and priests, which turned off heterosexual males from considering the priesthood; and, finally, a strong secular spirit.

As I noted in my book, *Brave New Church*, a booming economy and the enticements not only of extreme sports and endless entertainment and distractions but also, more to our point, of an array of exciting and challenging professions, are more attractive to the young than a religious vocation. So many paths lie open to the young man of today, paths that he can follow with an expectation of social and financial success. We read all the time how computer savvy kids are creating websites and racking up money working the stock options. Kids are contending with the syndromes of "sudden wealth" and "affluenza," not a call to the priesthood.

At one time, in a poor economy, the priesthood and religious life was a way out of poverty. But not now. Any stirrings of the MTV-watching, Lexus-driving, bungee-jumping, sexually active, high-spending young man to the priesthood may simply go unheeded.

Q. *Am I right is saying that the incidents of child sexual abuse, as horrible as they are, are not to be isolated from society in general?*

A. Yes. The whole issue of child sexual abuse by anybody must be seen in society's larger picture of the mainstream, overt sexualization of everyone, from infants on up. Just glance at the omnipresent television that, in the pursuit of ratings, keeps pushing the envelope on explicit sexual themes and nudity. We mentioned that the age of consent to sexual activity is mostly sixteen, with many places much lower, such as the Netherlands, where we said it was twelve. Regular sexual activity among the youth is commonplace: the Guttmacher Institute found that nine out of ten Americans have had intercourse before they are twenty. That includes your sons and daughters. One in six men, from ages fifteen to forty-nine, has genital herpes; in all, eleven million men have it. Half of all teenage boys from age fifteen to nineteen have had intercourse. This figure shoots to ninety-three percent for men in their twenties and almost one hundred percent for men in their thirties and forties.

Another sign of the times is a creeping assertion among some intellectuals that children, as one sex therapist said, "have the right to express themselves sexually"; this may include "contacts with people older than themselves." As always, the first step to changing attitudes is to change language. So such people propose the phrase, not "sex with minors" but rather "intergenerational intimacy." A new book extends this trend. It argues that American kids are entitled to safe and satisfying sex lives. The author got in hot water for suggesting, in a TV interview, that a relationship between a priest and a youth "conceivably" could be positive. She backtracked under pressure, saying that there should be no relationship between a youth and any authority figure like a priest or a teacher or a parent but, beyond that, kids are entitled to consensual affairs.

Q. *While we're on the subject, some say that the cultural revolution of the 1960s has some bearing on the present scandals. Do you agree, and if so, why?*
A. This thought brings strong reactions from some liberals, but there is some truth to it, I think. I remember well the "don't trust anyone over thirty" slogan and the "let it all hang out" attitudes. In the '60s and '70s, there was the enormous reversal of thinking, from an emphasis on the common good to a strong focus on "me"; my

potential, my feelings. The center of action and morality shifted to within the self as sensitivity training and self-esteem seminars invaded the seminaries and religious orders. The bottom line (which persists today) was that there was no objective morality. Sexual expression was self-defining and encouraged unlimited freedom.

I remember that Randy Shilts, who wrote so passionately on the gay life, consistently warned his fellow homosexuals that, in light of the epidemic of AIDS that was decimating the gay community, the promiscuous lifestyle was self–defeating. In other words, I think the breakdown of an objective morality, the emphasis on one's inner feelings as the measurement of behavior, and extolling the "freedom" of sexual expression certainly affected those brought up in that era and had a bearing on the current revelations. Note that most of the perpetrators are in their fifties, sixties, and seventies and they would have been in the seminary in the 1960s and '70s.

These comments provoke allied thoughts, namely, that a sex-saturated media—which offers us presidents compromising interns, senators hawking Viagra, Howard Stern and MTV, Hugh Hefner and *Sex in the City*—are wearing thin in their exposure of the Church for its sins and for being too forgiving toward bad behavior. A jaded society that offers us an "anything goes" moral code is looking more and more insincere in its insistence on zero toleration for the Church. A country that loudly promotes toleration of all kinds of "lifestyles" and lionizes corporations like AT&T, EchoStar, Marriott International, Hilton, LodgeNet, Time-Warner, Comcast, and other major corporations that have invested heavily in the multibillion-dollar pornography industry, is looking more and more foolish pointing the finger at the Church. Television—which offers us six times married Larry King interviewing five times married Mike Wallace, celebrity births without husbands, and Enron—is sounding more and more hypocritical in daily parading the ills of the Church before a wearying public.

I should point out another curious effect of the '60s. One-time avant garde young priests who bravely denounced segregation (Cardinal Law), supported the migrant workers (Cardinal Mahony), and led Church reform (Cardinal Keeler) got sidetracked as bishops into defending the Church. In the turmoil of the '60s, when Church authority was challenged, the birth control encyclical sharply divided people, and some 100,000 priests and nuns left to get married, the Church was very much under siege. These issues distracted the bishops mightily and caused them to give so much time to defending the enemy without that they neglected to root out the enemy within.

Q. *Do you think Rome will change the law of celibacy?*
A. No, not as long as the present pope is in office. In fact, he recently reiterated his stand that celibacy will perdure as the rule for ordained clergy. The cardinals, at the April meeting in Rome, did talk about celibacy but only to affirm it. I note that some of the hierarchy are still wary of any public discussion of it. A priest from the diocese of Pittsburgh, for example, was recently summarily transferred for telling his congregation in an Easter homily that the Church should ordain women and let priests marry.

Be it noted here that celibacy has been followed by many cultures since ancient times. To this day Hinduism, for example, considers celibacy an important virtue, one practiced by their supreme priests though not required of all priests. Buddhist and Jain monks take the vow of celibacy, although they can change their minds and leave without penalty. For today's jaded set who've had failed relationships, there is a book out called *Sensual Celibacy*.

Q. *You're a priest. Are you ashamed or hesitant in wearing your Roman collar in public?*
A. No, not any more than a policeman or a sailor is embarrassed to wear their uniforms after the revelations of scandal. My reaction is, why let a minority of wicked men define who I am? The people who know me greet me and even those who don't are affirming. They know a few bad priests do not represent the majority. If I hide, they won't know that there are good ones out there.

Q. *How are most parishes handling the scandal?*
A. My impression is that they are handling the scandal in line with their own image. That is to say, the parishes that have little life,

that just exist to provide services, usually publicly ignore the situation and the people grieve quietly. The parishes that are vibrant communities, however, where ministry is shared and collaborative and the pastor a good leader, openly come to terms with the scandal. It's preached about from the altar, bulletin inserts are provided, and there's an open-house discussion. It's above board, and the scandal is collectively met and talked about. I surely favor the latter because I think the more the issues are talked about the better. The more people get their feelings out, the more the clergy are sympathetic and apologetic, the better.

Q. *Is there anything that makes you particularly angry?*
A. Yes. I am angered at the corporate-like way bishops responded, which is to say, they sounded too much like politicians. Their words were indirect and generic. They gave round-about statements that seemed to indicate they were caught in some rather embarrassing gaffe rather than in a searing disgrace. They used vague phrases. I can understand any of us initially fudging when we're caught in something bad but it seems to me, as the situation became clearer and more ominous, the bishops should have abandoned indirect political, passive-voice language, come out as human beings, and called it as it is.

Q. *Why was Rome so slow to respond to this crisis?*
A. I'm only guessing, but let me try to answer. One thing is sure: it wasn't callous indifference. Look: in what may be a blow to our chauvinism, we must remember that America is not the whole world and we represent only six percent of the worldwide Catholic population. Our problems would not necessarily claim Rome's attention, which is attuned to the big picture around the world. Second, Rome respects the chain of command and if there's a problem the attitude is to let the locals handle it. There are neither the resources nor the inclination to get involved in local matters, and Rome follows that policy pretty faithfully.

Third, very likely Rome didn't really sense the enormity and gravity of the problem, and the pope's advisors did not bring the matter to him as being of great urgency until it became quite apparent that it was. Again, this was seen as an administrative issue that should be handled on the local level. Fourth, Europeans in general simply have a different attitude. They think Americans obsess about sex and that the pedophile issue is an American problem fueled largely by its lawsuit mentality, an aggressive news media, and a hedonistic culture. As we noted in the text, Europe has no large multimillion-dollar settlements. Their justice system doesn't work that way. So they see all this as another case of American excess hyped by an anti-Catholic press and lawyers who want to plunder the deep pockets of the Church.

Finally, there may have been some hesitancy in tackling the problem because there is so much polarization in the Church. That is to say, bring up the issue of clergy abuse and immediately you open the door to those armed with loud and insistent agendas of a married clergy, ordaining women, and banning homosexuals. No one really wanted that to happen.

Q. *What did you expect to come from the meeting of the American cardinals in Rome with the Holy Father?*
A. Before I express my opinion, we must note that some, from the beginning, were skeptical because, they pointed out, the very ones summoned to Rome, the cardinals, are part of the credibility problem. They've all had perpetrators in their dioceses and most, like Cardinals Law, Egan, Mahony, and George, allowed abusive priests to continue on in parish work. They were among the excusers and enablers. Critics say that to have the cardinals determine a solution is like asking the fox to make policies for the hen house.

Anyway, I can hazard some educated opinions about the meeting. First, the Rome meeting was significant because it signaled to the world, however belatedly, that Rome had finally grasped the gravity of the situation. The fact that other powerful leaders and members of the curia were also invited to attend underscores the determination of the pope to come to terms with the situation. And that, I think, is very important. It also gave the opportunity and the forum for the cardinals to have a much needed corporate dialogue as well as a chance to talk individually with the pope.

Second, it gave the pope a chance to speak openly about the

problem and this he did forcefully. He left no doubt as to his appreciation of the gravity of the problem. His words are powerful: "The abuse which has caused this crisis is by every standard wrong and rightly considered a crime by society; it is also an appalling sin in the eyes of God. To the victims and their families, wherever they may be, I express my profound sense of solidarity and concern." The pope also let it be known that senior Church authorities who looked the other way were blameworthy. It was noteworthy that, for the first time, the Holy Father used the word "criminal" in referring to the sexual abuse of children by priests. This signals that neither Rome nor the bishops will view the situation solely in moral or religious terms but in secular criminal terms, and therefore they will promptly turn over perpetrators to the law.

Third, what happened in Rome provided the impetus for what I think will be a uniform national policy (as opposed to individual diocesan policy) on handling abusive clergy. I suspect that even a "one strike, you're out" rule will prevail and canon law will be amended to make it easier to remove abusive priests.

I imagine the cardinals also talked about homosexuality and the priesthood, seminary training, and a quicker and smoother way to dismiss errant priests. In any case, we will see some positive steps being taken.

Q. *What do we tell the children?*

A. I'm not a parent or grandparent, but I would think at least three responses are needed. First, tell them stories. My mother brought over a lot of lore from the old country. One day when my brother and sister and I passed a slight remark about our pastor, Mom told us a story that her dad had told her. One very, very hot day the Lord Jesus and his apostles were taking a walk. The disciples were complaining. "Lord," they said, "it's so hot. It's stifling. We've never felt such heat. Our tongues are parched. We're going to fall over from this heat. We're going to die." And on and on they went. When, suddenly, around the corner of a house flowed the most beautiful stream of water they had ever seen. It was sparkling, cool, refreshing, delightful, inviting. The apostles lost no time in getting down on their knees and drinking to their hearts' content. "Oh, Lord," they exclaimed, "never have we seen or tasted such wonderfully refreshing water."

Satisfied, they continued their journey, walking around the corner where the water was coming from. They stopped in their tracks. "Oh, Lord!" they exclaimed in disgust. "Look!" The stream was coming out of a dead dog's mouth.

One should never explain a story but let it work its magic. But I imagine a parent spelling it out for a child. Basically, a parent is telling a child that God has not abandoned them. Unworthy ministers cannot frustrate God's grace, and that grace will still flow even if the conduit is wicked. God who loves them is larger than any unworthy priest. The second lesson is to tell the child that one bad person doesn't represent all. A bad coach, scout leader, doctor, neighbor, classmate—you name it—is just that: a person who is mean or who did wrong but not all are like that.

The third response is one I presume that all parents have already given but now, of course, it bears repeating: let no one ever touch you in private places and that includes (since most molesters, as we have seen, are family members) your uncle or aunt or sibling, cousin, or teacher, or even the doctor unless mommy or daddy is present. If anyone touches you, come and tell me immediately.

Q. *Can you give us some website sources for your references in chapter six which dealt with the sexual abuse of children in general?*

A. Yes: Dee Ann Miller's website is:

http://www.advocateweb.org/hope/churchsecrets.asp.

On female abusers and teachers see:

http://www.vix.com/menmag/scottwom.htm

On the sexual abuse of boys see:

http://www.myost.com/htmldocs/articles/sexabuse.html

If you want to check out the US bishops series of articles on the sexual abuse of minors by priests log in on their website at

www.usccb.org/comm/restoretrust.htm

There is also the National Organization on Male Sexual Victimization (NOMSV).

The standard study on child sexual abuse is *The Social Organization of Sexuality,* by Edward O. Laumann et. al. (Chicago: University of Chicago Press, 1994).

Q. *Can you suggest some reading on the subject of clerical and lay sexual abuse?*

A. Yes, there are books that explicitly dealt with the problem of clerical sexual abuse long before the Boston scandal. Some are:

Jason Berry, *Lead Us Not Into Temptation* (Champaign, IL: University of Illinois Press, 1992).

A.W. Richard Sipe, *Sex, Priests and Power: Anatomy of a Crisis* (Philadelphia, PA: Brunner/Mazel Publishers, 1995).

Thomas Plante, *Bless Me Father for I Have Sinned: Perspectives on Sexual Abuse Committed by Roman Catholic Priests* (Westport, CT: Praeger Publications/Greenwood Publishing Group, 1999).

Philip Jenkins, *Pedophiles and Priests: Anatomy of a Contemporary Crisis* New York: Oxford University Press, 1996).

Two books on child abuse are:

Kathryn Brohl and Joyce Case, *When Your Child Has Been Molested: A Parent's Guide to Healing and Recovery* (San Francisco: Jossey-Bass, 1996).

Douglas A. Pryor, *Unspeakable Acts: Why Men Sexually Abuse Children* (New York: New York University Press, 1996).

APPENDIX II

A Homily

Here is sample homily, culled from the book's contents, that may be helpful to preachers. The gospel on the Sunday I preached it—to standing ovations at each Mass—was, fortuitously, the gospel about Thomas and belief. This helped set the theme.

Keeping Faith

Second Sunday after Easter, Cycle A; Jn 20:19–31

These things are written that you may come to believe....

Perhaps it's just as well that we have this famous Thomas story about believing and faith as we, as a Church, struggle with the worst scandal we've had since the Church came to the New World. People are disheartened, angry, and weary of the daily headlines and exposés, appalled at the revelations about their priests and bishops they once held high on a pedestal. All is in disarray.

There is the loss of trust in the Church and the loss of respect. The Church has lost its moral capital. How can people listen seriously to the Church's teaching on abortion and chastity when its priests are unchaste? How can people take the Church's admirable teachings on social justice to heart when it has been unjust to pedophile victims? How can the Church's stance as a moral leader endure in the face of the scandals? How can people give credence to the Church's teaching on family life and on the care and the education of children, when it let its own children be violated?

As for respect, the press has relentlessly paraded the sins of the Church before the public. The mainstream magazines and newspapers have made the scandal daily front-page fare, and the tabloid magazines and newspapers have delighted in revealing first-person horror stories. The political cartoonists have had a field day pillorying priests and bishops with cartoons ranging from the vulgar to the salacious. The sins of the priests and the "corruption" of the Catholic Church have become the scandal *de jour*. The once vaunted respect of the Church has evaporated. Its priests, tainted by the sins of their brothers, feel the stares and suspicions of others.

It's enough to make the people, like Thomas, lose faith.

But you know what? The people haven't. The remarkable thing is, they haven't. I knew it was so when I spotted that headline in the New York *Times* on Easter Sunday: "Parish Embraces a Time of Hope, Not Scandal." It went on to tell about the parishioners in a parish in Wisconsin who, aware of and fretting over the scandals of so many abusive priests that have opened up the Church to ridicule and criticism, were in church to draw a renewed faith from the themes of Holy Week. A sense of deceit, abandonment, betrayal, and death was there as well, all too familiar. But there was also the resurrection and this was Easter, and indeed, the people were there to embrace hope. In fact, all around the country, the churches on Easter Sunday 2002 were more full than ever.

The remarkable fact is that, although sad and angry, the people are still keeping faith. Many simply love the Church and would never dream of leaving it. In the article, a few said their faith was shaken. Some remarked that a priest or a bishop or a cardinal is only human. Others were glad it was being talked about as many priests raised the subject at Holy Week and Easter Masses. Most often, people talked about the Church in terms of family and said things like this: it's a dysfunctional family and we've got to fix it; or, it's like arguments among troubled relatives, but no one's ready to disown the family; or, after all, it's Holy Mother Church, and even when your mother errs or you get angry with her, she's still your mother and you're bound to her with lasting ties.

I wonder if the bishops are listening. Do they realize that the Catholic Church is made up of such a stalwart, faithful people, who make better distinctions than they realize? I am reminded of a great man of decades ago, Frank Sheed, father, author, theologian, who was privy to many secrets in the Church. With an eye to history, he wrote on behalf of us all. Listen:

> We are not baptized into the hierarchy; do not receive the
> cardinals sacramentally; will not spend an eternity in the
> beatific vision of the pope. St. John Fisher could say in a pub-
> lic sermon, "If the pope will not reform the curia, God will."
> A couple of years later he laid his head on Henry VIII's block
> for papal supremacy, followed to the same block by Thomas
> More, who had spent his youth under the Borgia pope,
> Alexander VI, lived his early manhood under the Medici
> pope, Leo X, and died for papal supremacy under Clement
> VII, as time-serving a pope as Rome ever had.
>
> Christ is the point. I myself admire the present pope but
> even if I criticized him as harshly as some do, even if his suc-
> cessor proved to be as bad as some of those who have gone
> before, even if I sometimes find the Church as I have to live
> with it, a pain in the neck, I should still say that nothing a
> pope [or a priest] could do or say would make me wish to
> leave the Church, although I might well wish that they would
> leave.
>
> Israel, through its best periods as through its worst, pre-
> served the truth of God's oneness in a world swarming with
> gods, and a sense of God's majesty in a world sick with its
> own pride. So with the Church. Under the worst administra-
> tion we could still learn Christ's truth, receive his life in the
> sacraments, be in union with him to the limit of our willing-
> ness. In awareness of Christ, I can know the Church as his
> mystical body, and we must not make our judgment by the
> neck's sensitivity to pain.

He's got it right. That's why you're here this morning. I think
people have an instinctive appreciation of this truth. No one—no
pope, no bishop, no priest—can completely erase the face of
Christ nor undo his mission. Grace is still amazing, even among
the revelations of scandal. Renewal is larger than sin, faith is
stronger than scandal, hope is deeper than despair. Jesus is simply
too strong, too "risen" to be undone by a new set of Judases.

I think people like yourselves have that same unspoken belief
of Mr. Sheed when he said, "Christ is the point"—not this or that
priest. It is to your credit that, like Thomas, hurt by the publicity,

wounded by a breach of trust, plagued by doubt, scandalized by betrayal, you can still come here today and steadfastly say with Thomas, "My Lord and my God."

It is with such faith that reform and renewal will happen.

After Dallas

The bishops' meeting in Dallas took place after the writing of this book and it deserves comment. In some ways, it was the bishops' finest hour (well, at least compared to too many unfine hours). For two days the bishops, in full view of the public via the media, met to expose their sins, their shame, their apologies, and their resolves at reform. They were ready to meet this crisis without precedent. They readily gave interviews, listened sympathetically and at times wincingly, to the anger of the victims and the unbearable testimony of parents whose molested sons committed suicide. They debated, apologized, and made firm policies. All of this took place mostly in the open.

I don't know of any other group that has ever done this so candidly, so forthrightly. Journalists, doctors, lawyers, politicians, government workers, or celebrities would never willingly let themselves be under such full and often hostile scrutiny as did the U.S. bishops. And in a church that is famous for moving in terms of centuries, to move so uncharacteristically quickly is amazing. And they came up with something substantial, though unfinished in some respects.

Yes, the bishops may have been dragged into this meeting and yes, they deserve all the bad publicity they got, but there seemed to be a genuine collective determination in Dallas. I think that the gracious, honest, and gentlemanly president of the United States Catholic Bishops Conference, Bishop Wilton Gregory, set the tone. Here are some excerpts from his splendidly forthright speech given at the opening of the meeting:

The Catholic Church in the United States is in a very grave crisis, perhaps the gravest we have faced. The crisis is not about a lack of faith in God....The crisis, in truth, is about a profound loss of confidence by the faithful in our leadership as shepherds, because of our failure in addressing the crime of the sexual abuse of children and young people by priests and Church personnel. What we are facing is not a breakdown in belief but a rupture in the relationship, in our relationship as bishops with the faithful. And this breakdown is understandable. We did not go far enough to ensure that every child and minor was safe from sexual abuse. Rightfully, the faithful are questioning why we delayed to take the necessary steps....

Only by truthful confession, heartfelt contrition, and firm purpose of amendment can we hope to receive the generous mercy of God and the forgiveness of our brothers and sisters. The penance that is necessary here is not the obligation of the Church at large in the United States but the responsibility of the bishops themselves.

Both what we have done or what we have failed to do contributed to the sexual abuse of children and young people by clergy and Church personnel. Moreover, our God-given duty as shepherds of the Lord's people holds us responsible and accountable to God and to the Church....We are the ones, whether through ignorance or lack of vigilance or, God forbid, with knowledge, who allowed priest abusers to remain in ministry and reassigned them to communities where they continued to abuse.

We are the ones who chose not to report the criminal actions of priests to the authorities because the law did not require this. We are the ones who worried more about the possibility of scandal than bringing about the kind of openness that helps prevent abuse. And we are the ones who, at times, responded to victims and their families as adversaries and not as suffering members of the Church....

That's as honest and straightforward as you can get. Bishop Gregory then commended the press for its exposure, but he also took them to task for not reporting the good things the bishops have done and the reforms they have made in the past. He then outlined the reforms the bishops were making in Dallas. Significantly, Bishop Gregory said,

As we set about this task, we bishops are very conscious of the fact that we were not able to come to this moment alone, nor will we be able to complete it alone. We realize, as perhaps never before, our corporate need for this grace-filled opportunity of working more collaboratively with our devoted laity, religious, and clergy.

In other words, in the future, you and I, all of us, will have a part in Church reform. In fact the new national guidelines give the rank and file an unprecedented role in policing the Church. There will be, as we mentioned in the text, accountability—moral, political, and financial—and collaboration. The bishops had been warned. R. Scott Appleby of Notre Dame's Center for the Study of American Catholicism told them directly, "The future of the Church in this country depends upon your sharing authority with the laity," and they seemed to have embraced his words wholeheartedly. We will all be Church. Bishop Gregory's speech was, as I said, remarkable and I urge you to read it. We have, to some degree, begun to turn a corner.

Policy

Given the high level of anger at the bishops and the depth of feelings, it goes without saying that not all were pleased with the resulting policy passed by an overwhelming majority of the bishops in a secret ballot (239 to 13). The people remain of different minds, perhaps understandably. For example, one serious omission rankles. In spite of Bishop Gregory's exact enumeration of the sins of his fellow bishops in contributing to the sexual abuse of children, there are no sanctions for bishops who mishandled abuse cases. The focus is entirely on the priests. That's like penalizing the soldiers while exonerating the captain who gave the orders. The most the bishops would do was to declare that August 14 and 15 would be days of fasting and penance for themselves (others were asked to join in) in repentance for their abject failure to prevent priests from sexually abusing minors. They also made it clear that this would not be a one-time thing or even an adequate response for their part in the scandal.

Another omission that puzzles and angers people is that bishops who knowingly reassigned abusive priests and even wrote letters of commendation did not voluntarily offer their resignations to the Vatican. To have done so, I believe, would have powerfully underscored their sincerity and their public acceptance of corporate responsibility. That the bishops did not address with sanctions their own critical role in child abuse cases beyond some words of apology and a declaration of penitential days leaves a gap of credibility and a sense of unfinished business.

The policy adopted by the bishops bears the title Charter for the Protection of Children and Young People, and calls for each diocese to set up a lay-dominated review board to hear abuse cases. It also created a national committee to monitor the implementation of the policy in each diocese; Oklahoma Governor Frank A. Keating, a former FBI agent and prosecutor known to be tough on crime, has been named to head that national board. Further, the policy mandates that all priests and all Church workers, from teachers to janitors, who have access to children would be subject to background checks. Finally, any priest alleged to have abused children must be reported to the civil authorities.

The charter then comes to the heart of the matter. It puts forth an almost zero tolerance policy by stating that any priest ever known to have abused a child—even if only once, even for a single act, no matter how long ago—may no longer be a pastor or a chaplain in a parish, school, hospital, or nursing home or celebrate sacraments such as baptisms or weddings. He may keep the title of priest and say Mass privately. Period. Thus he is not technically defrocked which, as a practical matter, the bishops knew Rome would not accept, and it does keep the man within the priesthood rather than cutting him loose altogether where he would be accountable to no one. Still, he may not wear his Roman collar or say Mass publicly. Speaking for the bishops, Bishop Gregory put it this way:

> As Catholics, we do believe in forgiveness. We do believe in the power of conversion. An abuser who recognizes the profound harm he has committed and who has shown remorse can indeed be forgiven for his sins. He just doesn't get a second chance to do it again.

Those are sensible words that resonate with many. Rome is expected to agree and move swiftly—at least as Rome measures time.

Still, some demur and insist that any offending priest should also be defrocked, lose his title, and not be allowed to say Mass even in private. Then, too, there is fuzziness in the definitions. Abuse is too broadly defined as any inappropriate contact with a child, regardless of whether it involves force or physical contact, whether any harm is apparent or not. Does abuse then mean a hand on the shoulder, a hug, or a pat on the back or backside? Are such gestures "inappropriate"?

Precisely because of such ambiguities, the policy will be reviewed in two years and clarifications will be made.

Gray areas

Others—and I put myself in this category—feel that the bishops have too easily given into secular pressure at the expense of the gospel. Fr. Robert Silva, president of the National Federation of Priests' Councils, remarked, "The policy is driven a lot more by public sentiment than the principal of compassion." I would echo Bishop Howard Hubbard's words: "I would argue that such a proposed policy, understandable as it is from a public opinion perspective, is not consistent with who we are as a faith community that teaches forgiveness and compassion and reconciliation." The question is, what about penalties for priests who molested children decades ago and have reformed?

Look at it this way. As we noted, most of the priests who have abused children are in their sixties and seventies and eighties. Consider this scenario: a seventy-six-year-old priest, who molested a child some thirty years ago, repented, kept in close contact with his confessor and mentor, and has remained chaste since that one incident. He has, of course, been punished. He was publicly removed from his parish, suffered the humiliation of public exposure, sent for treatment, and forbidden to have contact with parish life or any situation where there are children. So what has he done with his life? Let's say that all these years he, a wounded healer, has been a caring figure in a nursing home ministering to the sick and infirm. He has anointed them, heard their confessions, celebrated Mass for them and buried them.

But now? Now he will be dismissed, forbidden the public celebration of Mass and the wearing of the roman collar. The elderly will have lost their chaplain. Where will he go? With relatives—living out his remaining days in a monastery (which will slowly be pressured to change its charism from a place of contemplation and prayer for those who choose to come to a kind of unofficial ecclesiastical prison)? Will his punishment never end? Must his ministry suffer? Is this the gospel, to put the arm on reformed and repentant seventy and eighty year olds, remove them from a fruitful ministry, strip them of the signs of their priesthood, and in their old age tell them they must, in effect, go into hiding?

I think here of John Newton, the man who gave us the nearest thing we have to an unofficial religious national anthem:

Amazing grace, how sweet the sound
That saved a wretch like me.
I once was lost but now am found,
Was blind but now I see.

In his parish church of St. Mary's is this memorial which he wrote:

John Newton, once an infidel and libertine, a servant of slaves in Africa, was, by the rich mercy of our Lord and Saviour Jesus Christ, persevered, restored, pardoned and appointed to preach the faith he had long labored to destroy. Near sixteen years at Olney and twenty-eight years in this church.

His sins indeed were committed before he became a priest, but he left us a heartfelt reminder that terrible and base sinners like himself can repent and do something decent with their lives. We don't, of course, have to turn to the last century to be reminded of this. One can think here of Jesus and his treatment of Peter, that wayward priest who, if you hold that he was ordained at the Last Supper, got a second chance at a fruitful ministry after the resurrection. And look at the other eleven priests, with their jealousy, ambition, doubt, abandonment, and denials: the Church might never have gotten off the ground if Jesus had followed a policy of "one strike and you're out."

A front page story in the June 17 issue of the *New York Times* brings us up to date. It tells of a Fr. Thomas DeVita, a beloved pastor in Michigan who, at one time and for only one time, abused a minor. He admitted it, repented, went for treatment, and has been an exemplary pastor ever since. He must now leave this parish, and they are traumatized. A subtitle to the story reads, "A priest loses his collar but his parishioners wear the hair shirt." Fr. DeVita plans to go to a place in the country where no one knows him. He jokes about selling shoes but in fact hopes to find a job that involves counseling.

I realize and appreciate that the bishops had to make a strong statement, knowing of the deep hurt it would cause; maybe that's the price we all have to pay to restore trust. Yet glancing at the compassionate ministry of Jesus, I just wanted to add a footnote of reservation.

I have one final, practical observation. In this book, I wrote about the critical shortage of priests and noted how the continuing subtraction of accused priests aggravates an already existing crisis. At the time I wrote that, there were 176 priests who had been recently dismissed in light of the current scandal (adding to the 350 who previously had been dismissed). The number of current dismissals is now up to 218; this number will grow as there are still known abusive priests who remain in ministry, as well as some 850 more who have been accused. Under this new policy, sooner or later they will be dismissed. Shortage will be too tame a word to describe this crisis.

Amen

For some Catholics, the wounds of the scandal go deep and anger at the bishops deeper still. They won't be happy until some bishops resign or are carted off to jail. Other Catholics are weary of it all. Some have left in disgust.

Yet there are others who see this scandal as another one of the many scandals that have occurred in the Church through the centuries; and they see the meeting at Dallas as a time of opportunity. They sense new life for the neglected reforms of Vatican II. They are eager to take Bishop Gregory at his word when he says that the bishops realize they need to work more collaboratively with the laity and the clergy. They are watching their bishops as never before, and the bishops know it. They are demanding better leadership. They are striving to make more parishes operate on a shared and collaborative ministry basis. I hope you belong to this group. There *is* promise ahead, a rising from the ashes, a new Church, a new Pentecost. Be a part of it.

Remember, Dallas was but the first attempt at healing. It will take more time and more meetings and more patience to bring this terrible matter to a conclusion. It will also take your input. You will get the kind of Church that you demand.

Questions for Discussion

1. What did you think of the bishops' meeting in Dallas? Do you think the problem of child abuse by priests was adequately addressed at this meeting?

2. Do you think that the sanctions are too lenient? too harsh? just right? What would you have decided?

3. Should the offending bishops resign?

4. Concerning the way the bishops have responded to this crisis, do you feel a sense of hope? of despair? of business-as-usual?

5. In your opinion, what will the post-scandal Church be like?

Of Related Interest

A Radical Challenge for Priesthood Today
From Trial to Transformation
William D. Perri

A challenging assessment of a revered church institutution. The author suggests that for priesthood to function as it must, transformation is essential. Covers many topics associated with the priesthood.

0-89622-710-3, 144 pp, $14.95

A Trilogy from Fr. Bill Bausch:

First Place, Pastoral Ministry
2002 Catholic Press Association Book Awards!
Brave New Church
From Turmoil to Trust

Bausch focuses on twelve challenges facing the church today and offers responses that can move the church to minister to parishioners of the twenty-first century. *Candid, balanced, critical....Provides a good map for honest thinking about the realities of church and our world in a context of the here and now....* Catholic Press Association

1-58595-135-8, 312 pp, $16.95

Catholics in Crisis?
The Church Confronts Contemporary Challenges

Addresses such movements as new age, fundamentalism, and "end-of-the-world mania" and examines both the negative and positive aspects of these movements by showing how a weakened church has difficulty meeting these challenges.

0-89622-965-3, 240 pp, $14.95

The Parish of the Next Millennium
Summarizes the social and cultural forces shaping our lives and church by examining where we are and where we might be going.

0-89622-719-7, 304 pp, $16.95

Available at religious bookstores or from:
TWENTY-THIRD PUBLICATIONS
A Division of Bayard PO BOX 180 • MYSTIC, CT 06355
1-800-321-0411 • FAX: 1-800-572-0788 • E-MAIL: ttpubs@aol.com
www.twentythirdpublications.com
Call for a free catalog